THE CASUALNESS HAS TO GO!

A Message to the American Church

SHERRY HUCK

REVIVAL HOUSE
PUBLISHING

For permissions, contact the publisher at
www.revivalmagazine.global

First paperback edition: February 2026

Edited by: Amanda Cheatwood
Cover design by: Amanda Cheatwood

Printed in the United States of America.

Published by
Revival House Publishing LLC
30 N Gould Street, STE R
Sheridan, WY 82801

ISBNs
Paperback: 979-8-9944266-3-0
Hardcover: 979-8-9944266-4-7
eBook: 979-8-9944266-5-4
Audiobook: 979-8-9944266-6-1

Dedication

This book is dedicated to the Lord…
May He be honored, worshiped, and glorified!

Acknowledgments

I have dreamed of writing over the years on topics that I live every day—raising kids, growing and maintaining a family, acquiring wisdom through experiences, etc., and never got around to it because I was so busy with everyday life. This book is the result of the Lord speaking to my spirit repeatedly saying, "Tell the story..." It's a culmination of dreams, visions, and experiences that were totally unexpected. The topic is one I am passionate about, but not one I envisioned writing about.

Mr. Huck, the human I love most, was on board immediately when I shared with him what I sensed the Lord was assigning to me. He prayed continually for me and offered endless support and encouragement. He, along with our kids, Aaron, Chris, Caleb, Samantha, Bailey, Kaely, Kindall, and Jonathan, and long-time friend, Anne, have read through the pages to critique, correct, and discuss my message, along with offering their input and experiences. In addition, my editor and publisher, Amanda Cheatwood, has also provided more encouragement and support than I could have imagined.

Not mentioned by name, but so very precious to me are a handful of friends who have supplied ongoing prayer, encouragement, and support as I have worked my way through this adventure, and I am so grateful to each of them. These are my people...my family that I depend on, look to, and trust infinitely! Thank you is inadequate, but each of them knows my heart, and each knows that I love them more than life. They are some of God's greatest gifts to me!

Contents

Preface .... *i*

Introduction .... *iii*

CHAPTER 1

Caught off Guard 1

CHAPTER 2

And the Journey Begins... 13

CHAPTER 3

The Journey Continues.. 23

CHAPTER 4

The Story Continues... 31

CHAPTER 5

Casualness…God's Will? 41

CHAPTER 6

When the Greater Vision Discards
the Inconvenient Mission.. 51

CHAPTER 7

Disillusioned...61

CHAPTER 8

The Prodigal..75

CHAPTER 9

All is Well...95

CHAPTER 10

In Closing...Our Lavish and Extravagant God! 109

EPILOGUE: One Last Comment............................121

PREFACE

I wonder how many will read this. I wonder how many will fall to one side or the other after reading the contents—either in disagreement and disdain, or in agreement that someone else sees and is expressing what they have been experiencing for so long. I wonder: will they see my writings as whining and complaining, or as valid and serious concerns that demand attention?

My conviction is THE AMERICAN CHURCH IS IN TROUBLE, and if we don't get serious and fall on our knees with conviction while submitting to renouncing and repentance, the real, Christ-ordained church will fail. Yes, I know we are currently seeing pockets of revival and awakening, but for the most part, the American Church—and more specifically, the American Charismatic Church—is doomed... It offers nothing more than a revolving door based on its arrogance and self-centered motivation for success!

I know of many intercessors... true and devoted intercessors... who are crying out continually for the American Church to be delivered, renewed, and restored. They are being led by the Holy Spirit to cry out with deep heart cries because the future of the Church depends on it. If the church fails, we have the promise of many casualties; some of those will experience the immediate consequences of a failed church, while others will experience eternal consequences.

Remember the story of Abraham and Lot? Abraham interceded for Lot when Lot was in a place of compromise and deception, and the Lord listened to Abraham's intercession for his nephew and family.

> *"But God listened to Abraham's request and kept Lot safe, removing him from the disaster that engulfed the cities on the plain."*
> GENESIS 19:29 (NLT)

Lord, hear the heart cries of the intercessors that look to You for intervention and deliverance. They cry out according to Your will...

> *"And when he had taken it, the four living creatures and the twenty-four elders fell down before the Lamb. Each one had a harp and they were holding golden bowls full of incense, which are the prayers of God's people."*
> REVELATION 5:8 (NIV)

INTRODUCTION:
Tell The Story

During the last few years, I began to notice changes in the church we attended and in the church at large. I read a book by Francis Chan, *Letters to the Church*, that spoke to the current failures of the American church having to do with man-made vision, goals, and implements that lost sight of a Christ/Holy Spirit-guided church. The points and concerns noted in his book confirmed and supported what I was seeing and drawing concern over, while articulating the specifics in ways that helped me have a better understanding of what I was sensing and seeing spiritually.

In the bigger setting of the church, some of the things I started to see were more of a personal nature, seemingly small and insignificant, and easy to dismiss. What I could not know at the time was that these things were factors of a bigger issue that was taking deeper root in the church and churning the waters for what we are now experiencing as great compromises and casualness that has made the American church a follower instead of a leader...

Casualness, the competitor with Holiness, was taking on a greater presence in the American Church, and it was/is presenting itself in every denomination, every campus large and small, and impacting every area of relationship with an Almighty Father God for the individual and the congregation. Sadly, the Church has still not discovered the two cannot coexist, and if there is no awakening with repentance, the American church is doomed.

> *"But be very careful to observe the commandment and the law that Moses the servant of the LORD gave you: to love the LORD your God, to walk in all His ways, to keep His commandments, to hold fast to Him, and to serve Him with all your heart and with all your soul."*
> *JOSHUA 22:5 (NKJV)*

And:

> *"Love the Lord your God with all your heart and with all your soul and with all your mind and with all your strength."*
> *MARK 12:30 (NIV)*

A long time back, in my earlier years of Christianity, I discovered this simple truth: outward expressions are indicators of an inward position. This truth has presented itself over and over in recent years as all of us have watched our country, our society, and, sadly, the American Church decline in biblical convictions, moral standards, and social graces, as I note repeatedly in the chapters ahead.

As I read Jeremiah's criticisms of the Israelites and the shepherds in the Old Testament and the critique in Revelation of the Seven Churches, I find myself tense with alarm at what is now going on in the center of God's people in America, paralleling those criticisms so long ago... As you read the following pages and you find yourself, like me, in a place of grief over the condition

of the American Church, stop and pray… then pray some more…
We are called to intercession: that eyes might be opened, ears might
hear, hearts might turn, and the Lord might relent…

> *"Then will the eyes of the blind be opened and the ears of
> the deaf unstopped. Then will the lame leap like a deer,
> and the mute tongue shout for joy. Water will gush forth in
> the wilderness and streams in the desert. The burning sand
> will become a pool, the thirsty ground bubbling springs.
> In the haunts where jackals once lay, grass and reeds and
> papyrus will grow. And a highway will be there; it will be
> called the Way of Holiness…"*
> Isaiah 35:5–8 (NIV)

And I am sure of this, that He
Who began a good work in you
will bring it to completion at the
day of Jesus Christ.

PHILIPPIANS 1:6 (ESV)

CHAPTER 1

Caught off Guard

The first of many experiences prompting me to listen and see what the Lord was revealing to me took place one Sunday when our daughter was invited to a local church with her dance company to participate in worship dance. The following is my journal entry after the service closed:

> The opening of worship with the worship team and the more experienced worship dancers was exquisite! I sensed we were allowed a very small glimpse of what worship looks like in the heavenlies. Other pieces were performed, but none of them compared with the opening worship. Those pieces offered enjoyment and insight into the skills the students were learning and developing, but the opening worship was deep, abandoned worship that entered the heavenlies. As they danced, I was captivated by the beauty and the atmosphere that consumed us.
>
> The sanctuary was filled with a great host of angels. There were sentry angels at every door providing protection, and I sensed a great hedge of protection around the sanctuary. I saw, as I had seen before at this church, the angels at each corner of the platform holding bright

white lights in front of them. This time, I also saw the great Commanding Angel, whom I have seen so often of late, standing front and center on the platform/stage. Once again, he gazed straight ahead, eyes never moving, yet he was piercing/searching the heart of every person in attendance, seeking a response.

The pastor came to the microphone, but before he spoke, I heard very distinctly in my spirit, "The **casualness** has to go!" I suddenly understood that the **"casualness"** must first be dealt with in the heart…the core…of the pastor, and the congregation would follow his leading.

When I heard the Voice of the Holy Spirit that Sunday morning, I suddenly knew the **"casualness"** had permeated that church and was creating a hindrance to fulfilling their call and purpose as a congregation.

For continuity and context, I need to add some background regarding what I saw. A year before, to the month, my daughter joined her dance instructor at this church to engage in worship dance during the worship session of the Sunday morning service. As I watched from the back of the sanctuary, I saw and recorded in my journal:

Above the platform, there are lights strung across it to create an ambiance. The lights are soft, not bright. The lights are low in the sanctuary. At either side of the platform stands an angel holding a bright light. Around the back of the sanctuary stand many angels, each holding a bright light. The Lord spoke, "This place has been a church on the hill with mediocre light represented by the string lights. You will soon be the 'Light on the Hill,' burning bright as a beacon in the low lights all around, if you will seek Me…"

Since I didn't attend that church regularly, I had no idea what the specifics were that charged them with **"casualness."** But the reprimand was significant and worthy of serious attention.

On with the story…

The small church we attended for the past 18 years—and recently left—has experienced many changes, especially over the last seven years. We were part of the United Methodist denomination and had exited the denomination and, ultimately, our campus because of the liberal and corrupt positions of the denomination. Shortly after our departure, our pastor succumbed to cancer and passed away. Our congregation struggled to find a new physical location and adapt to a new and very young pastor—physically, spiritually, and professionally.

The church leadership, including the elders, began adopting the "new" practices that were gaining popularity in churchdom and believed to improve the functioning church. We exchanged on-site classes and other corporate activities—except for Sunday morning services—for "life groups." The life groups were to take on the day-to-day functions of serving the attendees' needs in a small-group setting, as opposed to the corporate church being engaged with individuals.

Over time, we transitioned into a "model" that was focused on the call to "spread the gospel into all the world" (which is very much a responsibility of the church, as well as a noble and biblical call), all the while ignoring the ongoing needs of the membership, including discipleship, fellowship, hospitality, and overall family building—trading one position for another as opposed to merging and prioritizing the two.

In short order, our leadership was so focused on reaching foreign lands and teaching people through our various "schools" to become equipped and successful missionaries that they lost sight of the commandment:

> *"A new command I give you: Love one another. As I have loved you, so you must love one another. By this everyone will know that you are my disciples, if you love one another."*
> JOHN 13:34–35 (NIV)

Although our church professed a "family mentality," it did not hold to that profession from a practicing standpoint. There were very few corporate get-togethers for fellowship, and many of the congregants felt used for their resources (tithes and service) but not valued or loved.

With life groups being the focus, most (or many) attendees during Sunday corporate service would gravitate to the ones they knew from their life group and never venture out to others beyond their known group, allowing for a clique mentality to creep in.

Sunday services had taken on a position during worship that took me back to my pre-Christ years in the nightclubs—very loud music with the lights down low to create an atmosphere. The position was: the louder the music, the more spiritual it became. Taking into account those with hearing issues was non-existent. There was no consideration for our very young participants, which included infants and young children who had more delicate and sensitive hearing because they were still developing. Some parents had taken to putting headphones on their children to help offset the high volume, and some adults would excuse themselves during worship and slip out to the common area where the volume was less penetrating.

Our family had purchased and donated a decibel meter so the ones in the sound booth could better monitor the volume and adjust it as needed, but that was quickly ignored and placed on a shelf.

On another note, a casual mentality was seeping in, in a variety of ways, which was exposing itself more and more as time went on. The young pastor knew how to verbalize love and offer much enthusiasm, in part because his heart was called to evangelism, but he was ill-equipped in demonstrating value by way of relationship, emotion, or practical implementation in an ongoing and practical way that comes naturally to a pastor's heart.

What was once common fare in the church—i.e., visiting the shut-in or sick, offering meals to one in need or providing a meal to the family after a funeral, making a phone call to one who had been absent from Sunday services, or providing practical needs to someone in crisis—was disbanded outside of a life group providing those services to their members. Because we are a small church in number, in many instances the life group did not have the resources to meet the needs of an individual, especially if the need was ongoing. Additionally, there were those who did not attend a life group. More importantly, these symptoms were pointing to a church that had its priorities out of order.

To cause further concern, one Sunday morning during worship, I had the following vision:

> Journal entry... As I tend to see constantly now, the Commanding Angel—dressed in magnificent and regal red military uniform—standing center platform looking out into the congregation, eyes never moving, yet looking deeply into the core of each individual. On either side and behind him stand shepherds, but none of them has a rod or a staff, and there are no sheep. Each of the shepherds has a look of perplexity on their face.

I immediately began researching what I saw, and I found the following scriptures, among many others:

> *"Then the Lord said to me, "Go again and play the part of a worthless shepherd. This illustrates how I will give this nation a shepherd who will not care for those who are dying, nor look after the young, nor heal the injured, nor feed the healthy. Instead, this shepherd will eat the meat of the fattest sheep and tear off their hooves.*
> *What sorrow awaits this worthless shepherd who abandons the flock!*
> *The sword will cut his arm*

and pierce his right eye.
His arm will become useless,
and his right eye completely blind."
ZECHARIAH *11:15–17* (NLT)

I understood... The shepherds I saw in the vision had lost their flocks and abandoned their implements as a result of their wrong priorities, motives, and influential flesh—yet not understanding what was going on... thus the look of perplexity. I was gripped by the last part of the scripture: the sword (enemy) will cut his arm (compromising his ability to serve) and pierce his right eye (the ability to see clearly and righteously) to the point of blindness.

> *"The shepherds of my people have lost their senses. They no longer*
> *seek wisdom from the LORD. Therefore, they fail completely,*
> *and their flocks are scattered."*
> JEREMIAH *10:21* (NLT)

As my concerns continued to add up and more visions and scriptures jumped out at me, I discussed these things with my husband and my children. Each of them was also seeing what I saw and more. My husband had been the leader in addressing the volume issue at our church because he was personally dealing with it in an extreme way as a result of wearing hearing aids. My kids had been frustrated with the varying issues throughout the years, and some had quit going to church as a result of no resolve.

Wanting to get all the input and direction we could, according to biblical leading, my husband and I met with a trusted friend and pastor to get counsel, wisdom, and correction if appropriate. He listened and then acknowledged our concerns to be valid and legitimate and confirmed my vision as an issue that plagues the church today. So our next step was to pursue church leadership.

As per church protocol, we met with the church "liaison" so that we could express our concerns and schedule a meeting with the pastor and elders. In our meeting with the liaison, also a pastor, we listed our concerns and, in the discussion, we asked if he felt they were valid and had legitimate merit. He admitted to us that he, too, had had many of the same concerns and had also considered leaving the church earlier due to his own frustrations. He promised to pursue a meeting with church leadership on our behalf.

The meeting was scheduled, and on the day before the meeting that evening, I spent the day praying and fasting. I desperately wanted the meeting to be beneficial and productive. I asked the Lord to please go with me/us and to speak through us. I was surprised when He responded that He would not be there in support of us or them, but He would be there in the meeting.

He then took me to the story of Paul and Barnabas:

Disagreement Between Paul and Barnabas

"Sometime later Paul said to Barnabas, 'Let us go back and visit the believers in all the towns where we preached the word of the Lord and see how they are doing.' Barnabas wanted to take John, also called Mark, with them, but Paul did not think

it wise to take him, because he had deserted them in Pamphylia
and had not continued with them in the work. They had such
a sharp disagreement that they parted company. Barnabas
took Mark and sailed for Cyprus, but Paul chose Silas and
left, commended by the believers to the grace of the Lord.
He went through Syria and Cilicia, strengthening the churches."
ACTS 15:36–41 (NIV)

I understood… There is nothing in the scriptures suggesting either Paul or Barnabas went to the Lord asking Him to side with either of them. There is also nothing pointing to the Lord taking a side but rather taking no position by remaining silent. I was reminded that I often allow my children to attempt to "work things out" during disagreements and conflict so they might grow in interpersonal relationship skills and ideally build stronger relationships between them as a result. I saw the value of the Lord's response.

The meeting did not go well. My husband, one of our sons, and I met with the elders, pastor, and liaison. We laid out our concerns, although from the beginning of the meeting it was chaotic and confusing. I later heard that one of the elders had verbalized his dread going into the meeting to another congregant, which suggested there had already been discussion amongst leadership and a negative position was already established.

I also attempted to share my vision of the shepherds, and the Word the Lord spoke to me at another church concerning "casualness," and tie them into the overall concerns, but they were not received. Near the end of the meeting, the pastor said to us, "This church is going in a particular direction, and we will not change the direction for anyone, including you. We love you, and you can either get on board or you are welcome to leave." With that, the meeting was concluded, and we were dismissed.

We spent the next couple of days praying, processing, discussing, and pondering what our response should be. The meeting with leadership was on a Wednesday night, and by Saturday we had concluded what our position should be, so we crafted a letter to the leadership in response and sent it out via email. We respectfully withdrew our membership and said goodbye to our long-time church and family. Below is the ending of our letter for the purpose of closing out this chapter:

> In closing, we have felt that we have been "on board" with this congregation for the past 18 years. We have served on committees, projects, outreaches, special events, the Emmaus Board and Walks, taught classes, facilitated Cleansing Stream for a couple of years; our kids went to Brazil, Mexico, and Honduras with church teams; we have tithed and given free-will offerings faithfully, along with personally funding special events or needs; we have engaged in fasts corporately and privately for the church and targeted needs; we have committed to life groups—as participants and leaders—and taken our place in work crews. We have reached out to many in the congregation to fellowship with, ministered to individuals in times of need, provided food, visited those in the hospital, and, as mentioned in the meeting, we have had many

dinners, parties, celebrations, and times of ministry at our house over the years, with the motivation being we get to fellowship with our "family."

Pastor, we heard your ultimatum. We can either get on board or we can exit. We personally believe that although this church is making great strides and has some great opportunities before it, we can do more in preparation for what is ahead by attending to lesser obvious needs and interests of the membership to build and sustain the base. We also understand our perspective and convictions may not be the same as yours, so with that in mind, we will take your cue and bow out and look for a place where we can continue to serve faithfully.

The response to our letter came in a variety of ways. One elder texted us, commenting that we had valid concerns and inputs, then posing that if we left, who would continue the battle and pursue the problem issues? Others offered humble responses to our future absence. Some didn't respond either way. Congregants responded with sadness and disappointment when they found out. With that, our longtime membership and attendance came to a sudden and dramatic end. We were, for the first time ever, "churchless."

In their hearts humans plan
their course, but the Lord
establishes their steps.

PROVERBS 16:9 (NIV)

CHAPTER 2

And the Journey Begins

So, what do we do now?

The obvious next step was "shopping" for a new church home.
We chose churches that were well known in the area, with larger
congregations to start with. If we were to find a new home,
we needed criteria that would help us identify it. Aside from the
obvious—following the leading of the Lord—we wanted to include
some practical items, such as a place for our daughter, Kaely,
who has Down syndrome, to fit in and receive much-needed ministry.
I wanted to find a home that offered prayer ministry and hospitality
opportunities. Randy wanted to be able to enjoy and enter into
worship without the discomfort and pain of concert-like volume.
And the journey began…

The first church we visited was well known in the area. It would be
considered a "mega-church" for our community, offering multiple
campuses and a variety of services both on Saturday nights and
Sundays. The following is my journal entry:

> We visited the main campus. We went to the last service
> of the day (they have four—Saturday night and three on
> Sunday morning), and it was full, with maybe seating for
> a thousand. We sat mid-section directly in front of the
> worship stage, so we were able to take in the whole service.

Shortly after the service started with worship first on the program, to our right on the worship stage was a continual flow of baptisms—ten or so, I think. While the worship session took place, which included multicolored lighting and fog/smoke billowing lightly on the stage for an enhanced spiritual experience, there was a continual line of people being baptized, similar to an assembly line. There were multiple large viewing screens placed in the front of the sanctuary with the baptisms projected onto them so all could view and celebrate the baptisms as they took place while participating in the worship.

The service was quite orderly in that the worship was for a set period of time, then announcements, followed by the message that was also timed. Everything was done in a very orderly and timely fashion for a couple of reasons. There were multiple services, so getting one service completed in time to get that congregation out and into their cars before the next set of people made their way in was crucial. In addition, the service was broadcast to three other campuses, so every aspect of the service had to flow and merge with the schedule of the three viewing campuses.

The associate pastor's message was on marriage and its model of the relationship between Christ and the Church. The message fit in its time slot, and then the service was completed with a closing prayer, and everyone was dismissed. We found our way out through the crowd in the hallways that was also exiting, and with the help of on-duty policemen directing traffic, getting out of the parking lot and onto the street was streamlined and efficient.

This is the local version of a "mega-church." In large cities, the mega-church is much, much larger, but for this area, this church is the leader in large or mega-churches. They also have a large children's ministry, so kids could attend a service designed for them. In addition, there was a coffee shop and a retail store advertised on the big screens prior to the service starting, along with multiple programs and ministries highlighted on the screen.

As we stood in worship watching the baptisms, grief washed over me. Tears rolled down my cheeks. I saw angels standing on either side of the platform in front of me, along with strategically placed angels throughout the sanctuary, and I asked the Lord why they were there. He replied, "I place angels everywhere my children are." They were the "keepers" of the assembly. So, why the grief and the tears?

Although everything was orderly and pointing to worship and the gathering of the saints, it was man-made... orchestrated... and I sensed that. I would assume the planners and the organizers of the service and the church functions believe they are honoring and serving the Lord in their efforts, but I felt as if I were at Disney in Orlando, being herded in and out. Every detail of the campus was extremely polished—finished, upscale, professional, and state-of-the-art. Kids went in one direction, adults in another, making a stop at the coffee shop or retail shop before entering the sanctuary, where many volunteers were directing and assisting attendees to a seat as they came in or to an exit as they left. During the worship, some—maybe many—were lifting their hands in worship and engaging, but it was different.

I longed for depth… intimacy in worship… a prompting of surrender… the freedom to linger in worship if prompted by the Holy Spirit. Time, order, and schedule allowed for none of that. There was a "casualness" for the sake of accommodating a bigger vision and serving a grander plan that raided the potential for holiness and awe and abandonment in the individual and the corporate assembly. I saw firsthand and experienced the grief of what monetizing and commercializing the church looked and felt like for the purpose of serving a "man-made" vision.

My journal offers the events and description of our next church visit:

As is always the case when visiting churches, before arriving Sunday morning for service, the Lord spoke to me to pay close attention to what I would see… what He would show me.

This is a smaller non-denominational church, with a couple hundred in attendance, that has its facilities in a flea market area off of a main highway. We know the pastor and his wife, and we know a few members. We slipped in and found our seats about a third back from the platform. The sanctuary is long and narrow, providing three seating sections across the sanctuary. One section, to my right, was consumed by the men who live in Hope House, a drug rehab facility. Hope House is strongly supported by this church.

The service was similar to most church services today. It's non-denominational, charismatic, and given to worship. During worship, the lights were lowered, and the music volume was increased significantly. The following is what I saw that captured me:

During the time of worship, there were two Angels standing on either side of center on the platform. As everyone entered into worship, the Angels danced from the back of the platform to the front and back again. They were deep in worship.

As I took that in, I noticed to my right a continual stream of men going to the altar. As one would make his way forward to the altar, fellow men would follow him and encircle him in prayer at the altar. They would finish their time of prayer and ministry and head back to their seats while, yet another would get out of his seat and head for the altar, with other fellow men following and attending to him.

As all of that was taking place, the pastor stepped up on the stage and took a microphone. He began to share a word for someone in the congregation who needed ministry… very specific ministry… and invited him/her/them to come and receive. In short order, one came up to the pastor, and he very intentionally and wholeheartedly began to minister to that individual. All the while, everyone was engaged in worship, and the Angels were dancing.

The pastor finished with the one he was ministering to and stepped back into his place on the front-row seats. Shortly after, a woman went to him for ministry. While he so tenderly and gently began to minister to her, I could see she was sobbing and receiving what he was offering in ministry. His wife stood to the side, clearly interceding. As the woman seemed to break, the pastor put his brotherly arm around her and continued to speak to the depths of her need.

The rest of the service was typical, with worship ending and the pastor offering a message. I was completely distracted by the beauty of the ministry I saw taking place amongst the men of Hope House and the attentiveness that the pastor offered to those in need. He embraced his calling as a shepherd ministering to his flock. Both were quite beautiful, and I knew pleasing before the Lord.

At this point, we had visited two churches, each very different from the other. Obviously, we had not touched the surface of what was available denominationally or in general. We live in the Bible Belt with a church on every corner, so it seemed clear we were in for a surprising ride of experiences. In addition, because our Down syndrome daughter, Kaely, was a longtime student in a local Christian dance studio, and her dance team had been invited periodically over the years to dance in worship at different churches, we were familiar with varying church styles and brands.

The next church we visited was quite small, contemporary, and much loved by a young lady and her family, who were friends of another daughter of ours. We were invited to join them and give Kaely an opportunity to meet some of the young people who attend their young adults group. Again, my journal entry...

> The sanctuary seated 100. It's a small congregation meeting today—maybe 30? A single guitar player led worship, although instruments and a stage area were available for others to join. As seemed to be the norm in contemporary churches, the lights were adjusted to a low, dim setting, but the music wasn't so loud as to be overpowering; rather, the worship leader led us into beautiful worship.
>
> There were three angels on the stage, one to the left and two on the right, all dressed in brilliant white and radiating light. Angels lined the perimeter of the sanctuary. During worship, an elderly woman made her way to the

altar, kneeling before the Lord, and then entered into flowing worship. Another young woman joined her in deep-flowing worship.

When the pastor stepped to the stage to offer his message, two of the angels came behind him on either side. His message was profound, pointing to Matthew 26:17–19, an account of the preparations for the Passover, which included an assignment for a "certain man," never identified and yet recognized for his obedience in his obscurity. The pastor insightfully noted, "The result of our work is important, not the recognition."

We had now visited three very different churches with differing focus and character. There was more to come and much to consider and ponder. It was crystal clear that we were on a journey we never intended to embark upon, and yet here we were.

Along with our church visits, we tuned in to a couple of online church services and podcasts. How the church and Christian society were evolving…

Thankfully, when we left our church home, we had committed to remaining in our life group that met once a week at home. It was a small life group with only seven to nine members, but it offered us much-needed fellowship, accountability, study, and discussion that kept us engaged while we wandered in the wilderness.

Over the years, I have encountered others who had left their church home due to unresolved issues or deep offenses—issues that went beyond disagreement on new carpet color or other petty topics, instead issues or offenses that cut to the spiritual bone… issues that challenged biblical conviction… problems that questioned godly integrity or moral judgment. We had watched others quietly leave over the years with no understanding of why and only knowing, in many cases, they were loyal, devout, and faithful believers now gone.

In our present circumstances, I began to wonder why others had left… Some of those questions were soon answered.

The Lord is my shepherd, I lack nothing.
He makes me lie down in green pastures,
He leads me beside quiet waters,
He refreshes my soul.
He guides me along the right paths
for his name's sake.
Even though I walk
through the darkest valley,
I will fear no evil,
for you are with me;
your rod and your staff,
they comfort me.
You prepare a table before me
in the presence of my enemies.
You anoint my head with oil;
my cup overflows.
Surely your goodness and love will follow me
all the days of my life,
and I will dwell in the house of the Lord
forever.

PSALMS 23 (NIV)

CHAPTER 3

The Journey Continues

Our next choice of church to visit was a church about an hour from us. Good friends of ours pastored this church, and we greatly valued them, their Christian walk, and their ministry. They also have a daughter who has Down syndrome and a friend of Kaely's.

This church was more traditional in that the building was traditional in its structure. It was a beautiful sanctuary, open and bright, with large windows lining either side. A large platform faced the congregation with a worship team. Behind the platform was a baptismal, with large stained-glass windows illuminating the baptismal and the platform.

Again, my journal entry…

> The song "Amazing Grace" led the congregation into a deep place of worship. The pastor interrupted the song with a prompting to go to a church member who had been sick, anointing him with oil and praying for him. Others joined the pastor to gather around the sick man and unify in prayer. All the while, the singing continued softly. There are sentry angels at each door, and angels gather all around the sanctuary. Two angels stand on either side of an elderly man, across the aisle from us, who is in humble worship. I see a very regal and powerful Shepherd

standing center on the platform…

The pastor took his place on the platform to offer his message. I heard his passion… *his conviction*. His message was accentuated by his past as an evangelist, his current assignment as a pastor, and his foundation established by years of growing in sincerity and maturity in his walk with the Lord.

I have, for a couple of years now, seen a great Commanding Angel dressed in regal military array—uniform and weaponry. I see him specifically in church settings, and when I see him, I am also given a specific message that speaks to the church, the setting, or current circumstances. This day, at first glance, I assumed he was what I was seeing, but at a closer look, it was clear this was not the great Commanding Angel I often see, but rather, a regal and powerful Shepherd.

As I have prayed, asking for understanding, and pondered why I often see the Commanding Angel but this time a Shepherd, I was given the following: The Commanding Angel is placed in congregations to search for and encourage varying godly attributes and to offer protection against the enemy pursuing breaches in the wall: weak and exposed traits of the flesh, compromise, division, and the like. The Shepherd in this congregation was placed there to encourage and reinforce the desire and commitment to shepherd the flock. It was obvious that the priority of the pastor was to shepherd the flock entrusted to him above other responsibilities and duties.

A couple of weeks later, we visited another prominent and popular church in the area. This church would likely be considered a competitor to the larger mega-church we visited earlier. We joined the congregation just as the service was beginning. I immediately began to look, asking the Lord what I was to see. My journal entry...

> The worship was engaging and inviting. The stage was large, and the church was polished and well maintained, furnished with plush and comfy theater-like seats. The stage was equipped with professional lighting, large monitor screens, and a variety of instruments accompanied by musicians. This church obviously placed significant importance on its worship experience, as evidenced by its investments in every detail of lighting, technology, equipment, and decor.
>
> Ministering angels stood on either side of many congregants throughout the worship, and I understood... They had been discharged by the Lord to address individual needs, and ministry was taking place. I found myself wondering whether the individuals with the angels alongside them were aware of what the Lord was providing for them... Were they receiving what was so beautifully offered? This service somehow meshed together the man-created with the Spirit-led.

What do I mean by that last sentence? The service was definitively created, orchestrated, and implemented by a team of professionals, just as we had experienced in so many other church services, and yet there was an element of spiritual engagement in this service that was not readily available in other church services we experienced.

Our next visit took us to a much younger and newer congregation that held its services in a renovated area of a once-thriving mall in town. Their pastor was away, and a guest speaker whom we knew addressed the congregation that day. From the moment we entered the sanctuary, the atmosphere was different. My journal entry…

> Once again, the Commanding Angel stands front and center, looking, searching hearts and souls… Looking throughout the congregation, I wonder who might respond. There is a "casualness" in this place, stronger than other congregations we have visited. Worship consisted of a couple of songs. I didn't see many singing along, and only one or two people raising their hands.
>
> I looked to my left, and the five or six across from us were young, 18- to 20-something, attending to their lattes and preoccupied with their phones. As I pondered them, one young lady pulled a banana out of her purse and began consuming it. Again, I was aware of the Commanding Angel searching, and I wondered what he saw as he looked deep into the hearts before him.
>
> An angel stands on either side of the speaker, and I understand. They are to assist him as he walks and operates in his anointing and calling. His message was entitled "Rules without Relationship Equal Rebellion! The Church

Today." Once he finished his message, the worship team performed a closing song, and the congregation was dismissed. The speaker's message was on-point and very relevant, but I didn't sense that anyone heard it.

On to another extremely popular and successful church in the area. This one, like most these days, is contemporary and strives for relevance in the current wave of popular Christianity. Once again, this is my journal entry…

> Like so many of the churches we've visited, during worship the lights go down low, and a light smoke billows up around the stage. Current popular worship songs lead the congregation that fills about 75% of the auditorium. This service is the third and final of the day. Sentry angels stand on the platform and at each of the doorways. The worship songs were drawing.

Once again, as in other churches, I sensed the ministry's structure was built on man-made plans, vision, concepts, motivation, and current popular church models, although I didn't have anything concrete or blatantly obvious to support my sense. It was service as usual, and there was no real or deep reverence or devotion that would draw one in.

We visited two more churches in the weeks to come. The first of the two had been restructured in the last year. The previous pastor had passed away due to illness, and a younger pastor had accepted the call to lead. My journal entry…

The church is small and out of the way. There are about 25–28 people in attendance. The atmosphere is sincere and humble. I heard the Voice of the Lord: Rev. 3:8 — *"I know your works. Behold, I have set before you an open door, which no one is able to shut. I know that you have but little power, and yet you have kept my word and have not denied my name." (REVELATION 3:8, ESV)*

The sanctuary is filled with a large host of angels — six guardian angels — one at each corner of the room, two standing on either side of the entry doors.
Two "Keepers of the Word" angels stand on either side of the podium where a Bible lies. Two sentry angels stand with the pastor and two with his wife. The Presence of the Lord is here…

The last I will note for now is a church a couple of hours from us that is heavily engaged in addiction ministry in their area. We've attended this church before. My journal entry…

This congregation is small, maybe 50 people, with some of them being in rehab or pursuing restoration. This church subscribes to an extremely casual mentality that is noted and promoted on its website. The Lord spoke to me to look… As I looked, I saw:

Three angels stand on the platform behind the worship team. To the right and in the corner stands an angel dressed in white with eyes of sapphire. I understand;

I've seen him before. He's searching for transparency, but he sees through a cloudy lens. Transparency is not available; the hearts are not open or receptive.

The perfect church service
would be the one we were
almost unaware of; our attention
would have been on God.
But every novelty prevents this.
It fixes our attention on the
service itself; and thinking
about worship is a different
thing than worshiping ...
'Tis mad idolatry that makes the
service greater than the god.

C.S. Lewis

CHAPTER 4

The Story Continues

During the summer, while we were busy visiting various churches, I recorded the following dream in my journal:

Last night I had a dream that is worth recording...

Randy and I were standing in a large building, I think it was empty, with one side open. The opening was like a huge barn door or garage door that opened up the whole side. Outside was a huge open area, and Randy said to me, "They are here." As I looked outside, I could see many landing or materializing. All took on the form of people from the Renaissance era dressed in that clothing, brightly colored, ornate, and exaggerated. Some were in chariots, although no horses were pulling them. Others were descending on the ground, and I knew that although they were in the form of people, they were not. Instead, they were demons.

I found myself thinking, "How do we deal with these strategically? Be careful. Use wisdom and judgment..." They were coming into the building where we were. I then heard noise above us and realized there were rooms above. I noticed a hallway before me with a stairway at the end of the hallway to my right. One of the demons said to me, "She's looking for them."

When the demon said that, suddenly "idols" appeared everywhere, idols made of wood, metal, stone, etc., all very ornate, beautiful, exotic, even exquisite. I saw "her" stepping off the last stair into the hallway. She was clearly their leader, dressed regally as a queen, and as she came down the hallway to me, I asked if I should refer to her as a queen. She corrected me and said I should only call her by the first and last name she gave (I don't remember the name, although the name was average and simple, like Mary Smith). All the while, I was constantly wondering how to address the demonic activity with strategy and success. Suddenly, the dream was over.

What I've understood so far: The building was the church, although it was empty. The idols were everywhere and hidden in plain sight until they were referred to by the demon.

I understood "she" was the world. In the dream, she was alternately dressed in regal, royal finery, and then she would transform into a common, everyday, average-dressed individual. The world had infiltrated the church, searching for its "idols." The church was empty because the idols had led the congregants/members astray, and they had abandoned their belief system for the world's beliefs, causing them to leave the church to enter the world. The "IDOLS," being very ornate, alluring, and attractive in differing shapes, sizes, and materials, represented different draws in the world.

"The LORD replies, 'This has happened because my people have abandoned my instructions; they have refused to obey what I said. Instead, they have stubbornly followed their own desires and worshiped the images of Baal, as their ancestors taught them.'"
JEREMIAH 9:13–14 (NLT)

Now that the idols had accomplished their purposes, it was time to collect them and take them back.

I asked the Lord why the leader switched back and forth between appearing as a regal authority and a commoner. The Lord responded, "She was the Queen of Deception." She presented herself as needed for the purposes intended, all the while using her wiles (the idols) to lure her victims.

I was further intrigued when I ran across a current statistic noted in *The Awe of God* by John Bevere, stating: The Barna Group reported that more than forty million Americans departed from the faith from the years 2000 to 2020! Half now profess to be non-Christians, atheists, and agnostics. (Week 2, Day 4, pg. 67)

Church attendance among Christians has shown a significant decline since the year 2000. According to data from Gallup, regular church attendance has steadily decreased over the last two decades. Two decades ago, an average of 42% of U.S. adults attended religious services every week or nearly every week; more recently, that share is about 30%. Additionally, Barna reports that the percentage of "practicing Christians" in the United States has nearly halved since 2000, from 45% to 25%.

There are a variety of positions and speculations as to why the church is dwindling. Many or all could be accurate. At the heart of the problem, people are walking away from the church, and up to half now profess they no longer believe. That's terrifying! What does that mean for their well-being in a fallen and corrupt world? What does that mean for their Eternity? Depending on the doctrine one embraces would determine their eternity as interpreted in the Scriptures.

Of those who still believe and confess a relationship with their God but no longer have fellowship of any real meaning, I am reminded of the word picture given by a noted teacher I sat under many years ago. The teacher used an illustration of the animal kingdom. He pointed to the young, the abandoned, the sick, and the elderly in a herd. Any of these that got separated from the herd were potentially pounced on by the predators of that herd and destroyed. The same is potentially true for the ones who wander away from the Body of Christ without connecting with another family unit, especially if they are wounded, abandoned, or disillusioned. In the current church climate in this country, it is quite easy to justify avoiding another bad experience and thus not attempting to connect with another body of believers.

Additionally, for those of us who have left the church (at least for now) but have not walked away from our belief system, our relationship with our Father God, and our convictions, we are finding alternate ways to engage, invest, and participate in the fellowship of believers as we attempt to abide by the scripture:

*Hebrews 10:25 says, "...not forsaking the assembling of ourselves together, as is the manner of some, **but exhorting one another,***

and so much the more as you see the Day approaching"
(emphasis added). (NKJV)

Shortly after that dream, I was participating in a conversation with some long-time friends about our experiences and concerns in the Church. One friend, who attended a multi-campus mega-church in another state, forwarded an article published in *The Wall Street Journal* about that church. Here are some excerpts from that article: (https://www.mk.co.kr/en/world/11019629)

> In the United States, where thousands of traditional churches close due to a decrease in the number of believers every year, the "church franchise" model, which recently introduced a capitalist method, has gained national popularity and is expanding its religion.

> *The Wall Street Journal* reported on May 19, 2024, that a new "pioneering church network" is spreading in the United States and abroad, like a network of founders in Silicon Valley.

The article went on to note:

> "We need a pastor who knows how to lead the church based on market principles," stated one church pastor of the network.

> The success of this pioneering church network is giving new impetus to the American Christian community, which has suffered from a decrease in the number of believers who go to church every year.

"The pioneering church network is almost the same as Silicon Valley's venture capitalist model when it comes to growth," said Ryan Burgie, a professor at the University of Eastern Illinois.

The article addresses the church's developmental strategies to build church numbers and offers advice on "Search Engine Optimization" (SEO), which raises the possibility that the name of the new church will be placed at the top of Google search results or Google ad execution.

The article further states:

In addition, ARC evaluates credit scores, financial status surveys, marriage evaluations, social media account checks, and employee and volunteer management abilities to church founders.

I am not a business professional, but I do understand the value of a great business model to grow a business for the purpose of selling a service or product. It seems Christian leaders have concluded the need to pattern Christian growth and involvement after a secular Silicon Valley model to build attendance numbers and increase income. When we boil it down, it's all about the numbers and dollars a church can achieve.

Because of this attitude, these leaders view God's people as resources to serve their vision instead of seeing the vision as the vehicle to serve the people. The success of the vision justifies the cost of wounded lives and shattered people. Justice, mercy, integrity, and love are compromised for success. Decisions are based on money, numbers, and results. (Borrowed from *The Bait of Satan*, pg. 37)

What happened to the simple idea of brothers and sisters coming together to share the Word of God for the purpose of growing, maturing, and strengthening one another? What about the simple concept of Christian family fellowshipping, sharing life together, ministering to one another, supporting and encouraging one another in everyday life, resulting in a natural growth in numbers due to the Holy Spirit drawing onlookers in because of the beauty and intimacy of family they witness?

Has the American church fallen so far off the spiritual wagon that it has reduced its existence to a business model, or chasing after the importance of creating its brand?

A friend of mine recorded this vision in her journal, along with her comments (Wed., 12/29/22):

> "This was more of a vision than a dream but very vivid.
> I saw a beautiful gilded golden cage, and in the cage was
> a white dove. I understood that the dove was the Holy
> Spirit. I then saw the 'spirit-filled church' and that they
> would carry around this golden cage with the dove and
> proudly put it on display on a pedestal in the front of the
> church, announcing that this 'church' allows the Holy
> Spirit in it. However, the church would have its service,
> sticking to its agenda and time frame, never allowing the

dove to freely move within its services. 'Holy Spirit in name only.'"

Side Note:

I knew, at that time, that this was something I was to share with my church as it was directly for them, but I was hesitant to share. One Sunday morning several months later, as we met together for prayer before service, the pastor looked at me and said, "I think you have something to share." I remember hesitating and then responding, "Yes, are you really sure you want to hear it?" I proceeded to tell them what I saw, and they all agreed that it was a powerful visual of how it is in so many churches ... but I knew that they didn't understand it was specifically for them. After finishing, the pastor proceeded to say, "So the agenda for today's service is ..."

I know that this applies to many, many churches, but I continually wonder what my church would be like now if they had listened and understood. I pray that this word, along with other words given to them, will eventually be remembered and taken seriously before it's too late.

So, I might reiterate and add ... Has the American church fallen so far off the spiritual wagon that it has reduced its existence to a business model, or chasing after the importance of creating its brand, while pursuing its agenda? As I consider the vision above, I am reminded of the churches we visited that were controlled by their scheduled services, their perceived importance in synchronizing and choreographing every detail of the service, the need to manufacture and order the ebb and flow of the spiritual atmosphere, the value that was placed on performance and impressive communications.

Where was the Holy Spirit in those places? He was on display by way of the most popular worship song. He was promoted through beautifully articulated and polished sermons. He was referred to continually in the order of service via pamphlets, posters, posted scriptures on the big screens, etc. But "HE" was only on display, not actually available and allowed to enter into the service, not allowed to control the service, not allowed to actually minister individually or collectively within the confines of the service, either before, during, or after the service. There was no time or place for the interruption or the redirection of the service. My God … My God, where have we landed?

As we ponder those components of the failing church, we need to also include another component or two …

No man is greater than his
prayer life. The pastor who is not
praying is playing; the people
who are not praying are straying.
We have many organizers,
but few agonizers; many players
and payers, few pray-ers;
many singers, few clingers;
lots of pastors, few wrestlers;
many fears, few tears; much fashion,
little passion; many interferers,
few intercessors; many writers,
but few fighters. Failing here,
we fail everywhere.

Leonard Ravenhill

CHAPTER 5

Casualness...God's Will?

Before I jump into the conundrum of Casualness, it is important that I address a question I struggled with early on in my experiences of seeing angels in all the church services we attended. I asked the Lord, "Why are there angels at every service we attend, regardless of how spiritual or spiritless the service might be?" He was quick to answer with a very simple, yet all-encompassing answer: "I place my angels everywhere my children are."

Of course. His children are His primary concern, and His angels are one of His greatest provisions. Their presence isn't dependent on spiritual atmosphere. Rather, their presence is determined by their assignment. I would note here that this should also always be our reason for being present: because we are obedient to an assignment.

Casualness

When the Lord spoke to me in the church service that the casualness had to go, I understood, on a surface level, His intent. I immediately had thoughts of the extremely casual dress of church attendees, including pastors and other leaders. In many cases, people walked into a sanctuary looking as if they grabbed the first thing they found on the floor and threw it on, and then sauntered into the sanctuary with their latte and/or snacks so they could situate themselves in their most comfortable fashion for the expected worship show, very similar to the casual attitude seen in movie theaters. In addition, if they had kids, they would bring an iPad or two, many incidentals for entertainment and distraction, along with a multiplicity of snacks and drinks.

> *"Assemble the people, men, women and children, and the foreigners residing in your towns, so they can listen and learn to fear the LORD your God and follow carefully all the words of this law."*
> DEUTERONOMY 31:12 (NIV)

Or:

> *"And so the Lord says, "These people say they are mine. They honor me with their lips, but their hearts are far from me. And their worship of me is nothing but man-made rules learned by rote."*
> ISAIAH 29:13 (NLT)

The once-held position among adults and parents to use church service times to implement training and equip our children to operate in an attitude of respect, honor, fear of the Lord, and consideration for others is no longer present. These are just a couple of things that flashed into my head from memory when I thought of Casualness.

When I looked up the definition in the dictionary and considered the synonyms and similar words listed in a thesaurus, I was stunned.

I also felt a very real wave of fear in my core when I scanned the synonyms.

Oxford Advanced Learner's Dictionary

casualness (noun)

1. lack of care or thought; an apparent lack of care or thought
2. the quality of being calm and relaxed
3. the fact of not being formal
4. the fact of not being permanent or regular

Merriam-Webster Thesaurus, Synonyms and Similar Words

Disregard, nonchalance, indifference
Unconcern, apathy, disinterestedness
Complacence, incuriosity, carelessness
Recklessness, unawareness, coldness
Lukewarmness, lethargy, detachment
Hardness, callousness, insensitivity

Lukewarmness:

> *"I know your deeds; you are neither cold nor hot. How I wish you were one or the other! So because you are lukewarm, neither hot nor cold, I am about to vomit you out of My mouth! You say, 'I am rich; I have grown wealthy and need nothing.' But you do not realize that you are wretched, pitiful, poor, blind, and naked..."*
> REVELATION 3:15–17 (BSB)

How does it get any more direct than that!? And what about:

Insensitivity:

> *"Render the hearts of this people insensitive,*
> *Their ears dull,*
> *And their eyes dim,*
> *Otherwise they might see with their eyes,*
> *Hear with their ears,*
> *Understand with their hearts,*
> *And return and be healed."*
> *ISAIAH 6:10 (NASB 1995)*

Or callousness:

> *"For this people's heart has become calloused; they hardly hear*
> *with their ears, and they have closed their eyes. Otherwise they*
> *might see with their eyes, hear with their ears, understand with*
> *their hearts and turn, and I would heal them."*
> *MATTHEW 13:15 (NIV)*

And disregard:

> *"They worshiped the disgusting idols in blatant disregard of the*
> *LORD's command."*
> *2 KINGS 17:12 (NET)*

Hardness of heart:

> *"...being darkened in their understanding, excluded from the life of God because of the ignorance that is in them, because of the hardness of their heart;"*
> EPHESIANS *4:18 (NASB 1995)*

These charges, along with a multiplicity of other scriptures that include more synonyms of casualness, are alarming as they speak directly to me and us today. These scriptures, in addition to others not listed here, speak specifically to us as God's children, not the secular community.

So, how does all this add up to, and equate, **Casualness?** I came to realize in the days ahead that **Casualness** is so much more than baggy pants, eating a banana in a church service, or being distracted by a cell phone during the sermon. Those were merely outward indicators of serious inward attitudes.

What would be the inward attitudes that fueled a casualness in the heart of a Christian? What is the motivation behind the casual dress? Or the disregard for promptness? Or the lack of consideration for another? Or the pursuit of being comfortable to the point of compromise? Or the inconsistency in, or lack of, personal spiritual care and growth?

Casualness is the obvious outward indicator of a lifestyle common in our society, but it is also the subtle, the hidden, the justified, the acceptable, and the defiant attitudes and motives that tend to rise to the top of our internal priorities. Casualness is, in fact, one of the primary displays of our devotion to a greater god than the God of Gods we profess to yield to. It is, in fact, the **god of me**, the **god of self!**

Self-centeredness, the greatest god in this country, is a powerful and influential force! Let's take the topic outside the church for the moment and look at society in general today.

And the second is like it:

> *"Love your neighbor as yourself."*
> MATTHEW 22:39 (NIV)

Those who are younger have likely heard of, or read, historical accounts of a time when neighbors would reach out and help each other. It was the "neighborly" thing to do. It was common, expected, and taught as the norm.

For those of us a little older, I recall my grandparents gladly setting aside their daily tasks and chores to walk down the road and help another in the rural parts of Kentucky. A few years later, in the early 1970s, I remember living in Indiana as a teenager and getting a call from my employer asking me to come to work on my day off. I was 16 and a cashier in a grocery store. We had encountered snow the night before that shut the community down, and all the scheduled employees for that day had called in, unable to get out of their driveways. The roads were impassable and next to impossible to even find. The road crews were out, but that took time. My boss called me, hoping I might be in a better position to get to the store.

I wasn't a Christian at the time and, as far from an understanding of Christianity as I could be, but common courtesies, consideration one for another, willingness to be inconvenienced, and community were all the norm and common standards in our town dominated by factories and corn and soybean farms. Plus, I had a Mustang with a 3-speed manual shift. I jumped in my little Mustang, and in a while, likely a couple of hours, I shifted from reverse to first gear over and over again, each time gaining momentum and distance forward until I arrived at the store, which was about three miles away. For the very few customers that made it to the store that day, they were able to make their purchases because we were open and serving. As I look back on that experience from my 16-year-old perspective, I realize now what a huge part it played, subtle and fleeting as it was, in shaping my character development and maturing me as an adult.

The attitude of helping in times of duress and need is still present today, but not common, and not present with joy or enthusiasm in our society. Society has declined drastically over the decades due to a self-centered philosophy that has taken control. Sadly, in many churches, finding and maintaining a core group of service- and hospitality-oriented people to serve is next to impossible.

On a side note, in the church we were members of, hospitality, visiting the sick, and making phone calls or sending out a card as a ministry was disbanded. That ministry, along with other in-house ministries of the church, was distributed to the life groups to address their members, which is logical and reasonable to some degree, but what about visitors to the church, or those who don't belong to a life group? Or again, what about the life group that is small or lacks the resources available among its members to meet a need or needs?

We can trace the root of our loss of societal standards back to the casualness that presents itself at the core as self-centeredness. The god of self does not want to be inconvenienced or bothered. The god of self is so self-absorbed in its busyness and hectic schedules that nothing or no one else matters in comparison.

Recently, I heard of a life group that was asked to help a smaller life group that had run out of resources as they provided meals to a couple recovering from a hospital stay. The second life group responded with a promise to send restaurant gift cards because they were just too busy. The days of a home-cooked meal delivered and accompanied by a visit and a prayer are personal and "neighborly" expressions of the past. This same church declares a "family" position in the way it conducts matters, and yet imposition, busyness, and shallowness, to name a few attitudes, would suggest anything but a "family" conviction.

> *"Then He will also say to those on the left hand, 'Depart from Me, you cursed, into the everlasting fire prepared for the devil and his angels: for I was hungry and you gave Me no food; I was thirsty and you gave Me no drink.'"*
> *MATTHEW 25:41–42 (NKJV)*

And,

"But know this, that in the last days perilous times will come:
For men will be lovers of themselves, lovers of money, boasters,
proud, blasphemers, disobedient to parents, unthankful, unholy,
unloving, unforgiving, slanderers, without self-control, brutal,
despisers of good, traitors, headstrong, haughty, lovers of
pleasure rather than lovers of God, having a form of godliness
but denying its power. And from such people turn away!"
2 TIMOTHY 3:1-5 (NKJV)

So, we declare one attitude and operate in the opposite. We staunchly promote our family devotion to one another, all the while steeped in self-centeredness and lacking consideration for others. How does this conundrum portray the original tenets of the church?

But seek first the
kingdom of God and
His righteousness,
and all these things
will be added to you.

MATTHEW 6:33 (ESV)

CHAPTER 6

When the Greater Vision Discards the Inconvenient Mission

"A new command I give you: Love one another. As I have loved you, so you must love one another. By this everyone will know that you are my disciples, if you love one another."
JOHN 13:34–35 (NIV)

Even as I write this, yet another example of imbalance and loss of proper perspective in the church is presented.

There is a church in our area that has felt called to reach and minister to the greater geographical community. A few years ago, one of the elders received a vision that called the church to the Greater Appalachian area, which included regions not typically pursued by local churches. These areas were not easily accessible up on the mountain, and the living conditions of the people were consumed with poverty, addiction, entitlements, and "clannishness." They were a different people, operating with a completely different mentality that required ongoing time, patience, and diligence to infiltrate and reach.

The church sought a few individuals within the congregation who would be willing to lead a weekly ministry to this group. The leadership found a small building needing cleaning and renovation to rent and secured it. The ministry was born.

Once a week, a couple of young men would travel up the mountain and offer a cooked meal to all who were interested, along with Bible teaching and fellowship. Over time, those who "felt called" to commit on a weekly basis came and went. There was one, however, who served faithfully for six of the seven years.

Over the few years the outreach was supported by the local church, little headway spiritually was noticed. The few people who came weekly were fairly faithful, and the opportunities to minister were significant. Progress, although seemingly very slow, was made. Relationships were forged, and trust began to develop.

Sadly, as the church felt called to other greater ministries, the little group up on the mountain seemed less important and significant. At times, the needs of the people on the mountain were overlooked and disregarded. All but one of the servants from the church eventually felt they could no longer make the trek each week and provide the energy and devotion needed, so they resigned.

The mountain ministry had matured to a place of relationship that often required other needs to be met. The one who remained faithful would often drive up throughout the week to spiritually minister to an individual or help meet a practical or financial need. As the needs grew and interest in serving dwindled, the church leadership made the decision to discontinue the outreach in favor of other, more productive and successful initiatives across the border and overseas.

Sadly, the needs on the mountain continued to escalate. The one was the person the mountain people called because he made himself available. He continues to do what he can, where he can, but the resources of one person serving are quite limited. The people asked him to please keep coming and teach them, minister to them, serve them, and he did.

The church that had the "vision" to reach the remote local people chose to trade their small, local vision for a greater vision that offered them more return on their spiritual investments. That church now offers "schools" to teach missionary service and reports much greater results and numbers in this field of ministry, while the little inconvenient mission was abandoned.

Here is another example of the "God of Me" presenting its ugly head, disguised as God-directed ministry. The church leadership employed human logic and reasoning to determine where their resources and talents would yield the greatest return. Numbers and dollars are, after all, the bottom line and speak powerfully in any human or corporate venture as to real personal success.

Love one another is conditional. We justify "love one another" when it's economically expedient or offers a great return that can be documented for all to see, including God. We are so proud of ourselves, in a very humble way, of course, when we can show the world and God what great servants we are, based on our definition of success and outcome.

In the early days of that small ministry, the now-deceased pastor oversaw the various people and services they offered on the mountain. The one who developed a great loyalty and devotion to the ministry asked his mom, one who often saw things in the spiritual realm as the Lord allowed, to come with him on a drive up the mountain to "see" what the Lord might allow her in the spirit. The following is her journal entry submitted to the pastor:

That day was cold, rainy, and dreary. As we drove up the mountain on a narrow two-lane road with the sky overcast, low-hanging fog all around us, and mist or rain coming down, I looked out the passenger window. I could see into the woods that lined the road and traveled straight up the mountain.

My spiritual gaze caught sight of demons running in the woods alongside us and up into the mountain. The only thing I could liken the demons' appearance to was the description of gargoyles I had read about. They never came near us, but running alongside our travels, they would hiss and snarl and growl at us.

As we drove up the mountain, we came to a bend in the road. In the bend was a large white building, broken down and maybe abandoned, sitting in the middle of a large, unkempt yard. Suddenly, I saw women and children coming up from the grave crying, sobbing, pleading for help, silently, once upon a time, due to the abuse and horrible violations, sexual and otherwise, they had encountered by those overseeing them.

My son asked me what I was seeing, so I told him. He explained that the building was once the home of a church and a Masonic Lodge that had a reputation for misconduct and abuses.

Soon, we came to a clearing with a house to the left, a couple of older mobile homes in the distance to my right, and in front of the mobile homes stood a small, old concrete building in desperate need of repairs and other attention. Even so, the small building, despite the dreariness, rain, and fog, had a halo of light consuming it. The light radiated from the building and the property, and I noted the light ended at the perimeter of the yard around the building. I asked if that was the church building, recently acquired. "Yes," he responded.

As I continued to look around, I noticed an old, run-down mobile home behind the small building. I saw death there, heart-wrenching death. As I explained what I saw, he told me a lonely, neglected older man had passed away there all alone in recent days.

All around the little building, outside the perimeter of light, was a heavy spiritual smog comprised of brokenness, defeat, hopelessness, great and overwhelming hopelessness, failure, violence, anger, and deep, dark depression.

Based on this report to the pastor, along with other inputs highlighting the need and the dire state of the community, the ministry was fully supported and funded at that time and continued for the next five years. The pastor passed away a year or so after that spiritual encounter, and a new, younger pastor took office. The ministry continued for another four years or so, but larger and more influential ministry opportunities were emerging.

The young pastor and elders showed less and less interest and concern for the mountain ministry, all the while the needs were becoming increasingly complex and challenging, with seemingly little positive results. There were three: an aging couple and the one who remained faithful to the mountain ministry. But the strain of the issues, the long and treacherous drive up and back each week, especially during the winter months, along with some health issues of the aging couple, led them to opt to retire their service. The one was left.

A few weeks before the older couple retired, another life group within the church volunteered to visit the weekly meeting on the mountain. While there that evening, the same woman who had experienced the spiritual insights some years before, and who was part of the visiting life group, went out and walked around the property, asking the Lord to show her what He would have her see. Again, her journal entry:

> Tonight, our life group visited the mountain ministry for the weekly meeting. Today, before our planned visit, I spent time in prayer in preparation for our visit. I repeatedly saw the building and property. Each time the building and property were illuminated with a brilliant light, much brighter than I saw some years back.
>
> As we drove up the mountain, I looked, but I didn't see the demons in the woods. After we got to the church building, I walked around the property. I asked the Lord what He would show me.

I could see the brilliant light radiating from the building and property. I could also see the light stopping at the perimeter of the property and darkness picking up from there. As I looked into the woods lining the property, I could hear the rustling of leaves on the ground and in the treetops. And I understood. The demons, still in the area, no longer took form but remained in the woods, causing the rustling.

The light, now much brighter than before, had gained power and influence, diminishing the power and influence of the demonic strongholds present, pushing back the darkness.

Then I had more understanding. The three faithful individuals have had a profound impact here. They have attended weekly for the last few years, cultivating relationships, ministering to those in need, attending to issues, sharing the gospel, and praying with and for the people, the community.

Their commitment and diligence have served powerfully to diminish the power and influence of the enemy. I understood their faithfulness and diligence have increased the depth and brilliance of the light while weakening the strongholds that have dominated and ruled that area. Their ongoing presence and faithfulness have proved to be incredibly powerful and successful in the ongoing battle for spiritual dominance.

Shortly after that visit, the older couple made the decision to retire from their service. The church offered leadership to the one, but due to some irreconcilable differences regarding biblical teachings and other differences within the church, the one rejected their offer and withdrew his membership from the church. The mountain ministry was disbanded and shut down. The church had too many other ministry irons in the fire and concluded this ministry was not a calculable investment.

They did not, for whatever reason, recognize or realize the tremendous accomplishments gained in the spiritual realm, and saw it as nothing more than a drain on their financial, practical, and spiritual budget.

Even so, the needs didn't stop on the mountain, simply because it was inhabited by humans — humans suffering, struggling, in dire need spiritually, practically, emotionally, financially, physically, and so on. Many of them cried out for help as crisis after crisis presented. They still had one number in their phone contacts that they knew they could call and get an appropriate response. He answered every time.

> *"He comforts us in all our troubles so that we can comfort others. When they are troubled, we will be able to give them the same comfort God has given us."*
> 2 CORINTHIANS 1:4 (NLT)

One resident suddenly became sick, a long-time addict, and was admitted to the local hospital. The one visited him faithfully, sitting with him, unresponsive, long into the night until he passed away. A small service was arranged in the basement of the funeral home with just a sheet draped over him while the one and a couple of other friends spoke a few words over him before his cremation, closing out his 50 or so years of brokenness and failure, likely to be remembered by no one.

A couple who had been more faithful than the rest on the mountain, attending meetings and staying engaged, also ran into a crisis. The husband had a massive stroke the first night on his new job of pizza delivery, landing him in the hospital and rehab for months. The family was already in financial straits, living day to day. The stroke broke the camel's back. They were in danger of losing what they had. The one answered the calls, found others who could and would help in small ways financially, and personally assisted with practical needs wherever possible.

Meanwhile, the church moved on, pursuing other ministries that, according to their social media posts, are much more successful and rewarding, offering valid returns on their spiritual, practical, and financial investments. I wonder how those human conclusions are recorded in Heaven and align with the scripture below.

> *"In everything I did, I showed you that by this kind of hard work we must help the weak, remembering the words the Lord Jesus himself said: 'It is more blessed to give than to receive.'"*
> *Acts 20:35 (NIV)*

We are living in an unprecedented time in history. America is crumbling from within, and the church seems to have little, if any, concern about it. The average church leader is more concerned about tithes and attendance than they are about Christ, character, and conquest. The early church turned the world upside down; now we see the world turning the church upside down. The church has lost her power, purity, and passion, which can be largely attributed to her loss of prayer.

LEONARD RAVENHILL

CHAPTER 7

Disillusioned

Forty-seven years ago, I became a Christian through a series of dramatic and profound experiences. From the moment I gave my heart to the Lord, I was forever changed. I immediately began searching for a church to join, and from that time on, I was actively involved in a church: attending Sunday services and other weekly meetings, Bible studies, small groups, and serving on various teams. I intuitively understood the value and importance of being engaged, active, and discipled. At home, I regularly studied my Bible, spent time in prayer, journaled, and sought the insight and wisdom of other experienced Christians.

Over the years, I've heard of and witnessed church splits. I've watched church members come and go. I've observed long-time members leave out of frustration, anger, and hurt over a wide variety of issues and problems. A few years ago, our family also played a part in the departure of a denomination when our congregation, like many others, voted to leave the United Methodist Church due to its apostasy, compromise, and corruption. We, like other long-time Christians, have seen the rise and fall of congregations. We have watched in disbelief as prominent and successful Christians have been exposed in their corruption, lies, and scandals on a national level, reported on the news for all to see. I have known other Christians throughout the years who have quietly left their church home in disillusionment and disappointment, never reconnecting in another church setting. Some have maintained their relationship with the Lord in some degree of loneliness and isolation, while others have eventually wandered away from all ties to their Christian beliefs and relationship with our Lord.

Even with my experiences and background in the American Church, it never occurred to me, or to us as a family, that we could find ourselves in such a place of disillusionment, disappointment, and despair. In the weeks and months after we departed from our church home, we were blindsided by the stark reality of the current conditions of the "church" at large as we visited and talked with others in various congregations and denominations. We were also stunned by some of the communications we received from the leadership of the church we left, along with comments from church members.

Going back to the beginning of our story, after we had the meeting with the leadership of our church, we found ourselves trying to make sense of all that we had experienced and heard from our leaders.

As I noted in chapter one, the Liaison had clearly stated to us in our initial meeting that he, too, had struggled with the same issues we were struggling with, along with some other undisclosed issues. I asked him specifically in our meeting where we were wrong in our concerns and frustrations. He told us in no uncertain terms we were on target. In our corporate meeting, however, he offered no input and remained silent.

In addition, another Elder privately texted me after they received our letter of resignation with the following: "Some of your concerns had merit, but without you there to lead, there will be no corrective actions taken. You are the only ones speaking up." Based on hearsay, when others left the church after us, their departure was credited to us. Because we live in a smaller community, we periodically ran across others who had left our church over the years, but we never knew why. Once they heard we had left, news travels fast in the church world, they offered more insight into their departure, and sadly, all the stories were basically the same as ours. They raised valid concerns, and not only were their concerns dismissed, so were they.

In the months that followed, we lost motivation in wanting to find a new church home. Disillusionment found a home in our emotions. As I noted in earlier chapters, we visited a variety of campuses and were surprised... shocked at times... dismayed...disappointed... and often entertained. We discovered a couple of churches that we believed we would greatly enjoy, fit in with, and have the opportunity to serve in, but due to the travel distance, about an hour, we couldn't organize our weekly schedules to support multiple activities throughout the week.

In the meantime, we enjoyed our Life Group with a few others, and we have abided with joy in the command to:

> *"And let us consider how we may spur one another on toward love and good deeds, not giving up meeting together, as some are in the habit of doing, but encouraging one another— and all the more as you see the Day approaching."*
> *HEBREWS 10:24-25 (NIV)*

And:

"They devoted themselves to the apostles' teaching and
to fellowship, to the breaking of bread and to prayer."
ACTS 2:42 (NIV)

We met regularly to fellowship, pray, study, or listen to a teaching by a well-known and established teacher through an online or book study, and we always had a great dessert and refreshments. Additionally, we made an effort to be consistent in taking Communion when we gathered and to stay in touch throughout the week. Like Randy and me, some of the members didn't have a Sunday church home, while others did. Regardless of whether we had a church home or not, all of us were grappling with the church issues of the day that seemed to be plaguing the greater Body....

As of this writing, we have been without a church home for a little over a year. During the last year, along with the rest of society, we have watched several prominent Christian leaders fall, a large and well-known ministry face scandal, and a Christian TV network teeter on disarray and potential collapse, to name a few. Those are on a larger scale. What about all the smaller and less influential ministries and churches that will fail and disintegrate, and that we will never personally hear about? Why is this happening? Why, aside from the obvious that Christianity consists of humans, are Christianity and the American Church in such disarray?

I found the following on ChurchLEADERSHIP.org which demands consideration:

Church Leadership

Why Churches Fail: Part I
By Dr. Richard J. Krejcir

The problems of the Church can be solved and used for His glory!

"The LORD is my light and my salvation, whom shall I fear? The LORD is the stronghold of my life, of whom shall I be afraid?"
PSALM 27:1 (NIV)

I was teaching at a pastor's conference recently. So many pastors were literally crying on my shoulder because of the overwhelming problems they face. This is no surprise; usually, I am the one crying! However, the surprise here was the focus (or the lack thereof) from these pastors. Most of them did not consider effective Bible teaching or discipleship important for their church. Furthermore, discipleship was considered useful for attracting people, not for mentoring and teaching them. Most of them did not think prayer was important; rather, it was about crafting a catchy sermon with a catchy title to draw people into their church. And, it gets worse from there.

When I led a workshop on "Biblical Church Growth," I spent some Q & A time with these pastors. And of course, they had "real" reasons why their churches were declining and in decay. One was the trend that since the early 70s, white, Protestant churches are no longer vogue in American culture. Many cited statistics and research about how churches grow only when the pastors can attract congregational members with similar attitudes or connect with church members during times of crisis and life changes (which are valid and effectual reasons, but miss the main point). And, most felt that prayer and even faith decisions are deep, nevertheless personal and not an essential component to building a church. And yes, this was for a main-line church conference.

I challenged them with my statistics on why churches failed. It was like I was speaking with three heads. Prayer, Bible literacy and its relevance, and discipleship were considered juvenile to them. Yes, their despair was sincere; they just could not make the connection that real church development has to do with focusing on who the church is for, and that is Christ! Most thought the church was for their own amusement and agendas. Seriously, how do pastors miss the point so significantly?

In my first doctoral dissertation on "why churches fail," I tracked over 1,000 churches for over 10 years. I looked for the marks that caused people to leave. I found the top four reasons why a churchgoer leaves their church.

1. The number one reason why people stop coming to any given church (your church) was reported by over 91% people citing the significant factor or main reason being conflict and gossip! (James 3:5-6)

2. The number two reason that people leave a church is the hypocrisy and judgmental attitude and actions of people. Seventy-eight percent (78%) of people who left a church stated they experienced church people being judgmental to them, the hypocrisy they witnessed especially by pastors and leadership, or the hurt by church members they experienced. Another significant factor in this category was the poor "people skills" of the pastor and/or leadership! Why? Because they do not manage the judgmentalism, conflicts and/or gossip! (Matthew 5:9)

3. The number three reason why people leave a church is because they wonder, where do I fit in? They experience a lack of hospitality and concern or care from the leadership or people in general. Sixty-six percent (66%) reported that if people do not feel they belong, they leave. (2 Corinthians 5:20)

4. The number four reason why people leave a church is
the unwillingness to deal with sin. This creates strife
and factions in a church for which sixty-two percent
(62%) of people reported to be the reason they left.
The atmosphere of contention they feel is the primary
basis for factions, the dissatisfaction, disagreements, and
dissention (if they stay), all because they do not feel at
"home," having a place to care and to share. Thus, the
poor "people skills" of the leadership, the unwillingness
to deal with and resolve conflict, and the lack of seeking
Christ first and foremost cause the majority of conflicts
between the people in the church and the pastor.
(Matthew 6:33)

These top four problems cause the vast majority of
people to leave a church, over ninety-one percent (91%):
unresolved conflict, gossip, no teaching, and inhospitality
that prevent "connection." (This statistic discounts people
who move for a job or school change, which is around
nineteen percent (19%); this was removed from statistical
relevance in the percentage hierarchy.) Over ninety
percent (90%) of people surveyed and interviewed felt
a significant, overwhelming lack of courtesy, absence of
Fruit, and bad character that led to broken relationships
and the flight from their church. Over eighty-five percent
(85%) reported no one ever called, visited them, or asked

why they left within the first four months after leaving. Eighty-two percent (82%) stated that if they were visited and given a reason and/or an apology, resolving the conflict or action was taken to resolve it, they would return. Over seventy percent (70%) of them were in leadership of some kind, and thirteen percent (13%) were pastors! These reasons led to over ninety percent (90%) feeling shunned, feelings of rejection, and/or not feeling wanted or cared for there. This prevented them from getting anything significant or spiritual out of church, so they left.

My personal observations were simple; Ephesians 4:1 - 5:2 was not applied or sought by the leadership. This comes from a lack of quality, biblical understanding from the leadership. This Bible illiteracy and feeling that it is not relevant resulted in a lack of quality expository or exegetical Bible teaching. In addition, discipleship was not considered important nor was Fruit being modeled by the church leadership.

Of the churches and people surveyed and tracked that were satisfied and healthy, the Bible was taught effectively, the church was healthy, and when problems came, they were met and turned into happenings of connection and learning. After that, the congregation was better able and willing to put God's precepts in practice with real, authentic Christian character and faith. Problem churches turned around and factions ended simply by seeking Christ first. It starts from the leadership. People do not know the Word or the precepts of our Lord because the Bible is not taught in such a way that it is real and can be applied to their lives and situations. Sheep who are not being fed will feed upon one another and not love one another! The Church is called—*even mandated*—to equip and disciple its people, not just in the basics of the faith, but also in how to be Christian in their families, work, school, and relationships. When churches do not engage in this vital call, they create ineffective Christians who do not seek to live their lives to His glory (Psalm 119:9-12)! After a while, the church stagnates to nothing and eventually will close its doors.

We dealt with so many of the specifics mentioned. We experienced the frustration of "cliques" among the leadership in our church. There was often a prevailing attitude of superiority and elitism in the hierarchy of leadership. I watched and mused over countless lay people meeting with leadership, asking to start a new ministry or group, only to be rejected. And yet, often shortly after that idea or suggestion was dismissed, a member of the leadership would initiate the same ministry or group that had been rejected. I observed, on occasion, gossip flourish among the leadership, with a leak from time to time, causing the subject of the gossip to find out and leave the church. As mentioned in our original concerns with the Elders, discipleship was discontinued with the replacement of life groups. Again, there is a valid and beneficial place for life groups, but they are not a one-size-fits-all provision. Hospitality, as we once enjoyed it, was discontinued. In its place, a mediocre and random time of church-wide fellowship ensued, if at all. Again, every need within the church body was redirected to the life group, which left no place for corporate fellowship outside of the Sunday morning service.

> *"And let us consider how to stir up one another to love and*
> *good works, not neglecting to meet together, as is the habit of*
> *some, but encouraging one another, and all the more as you see*
> *the Day drawing near."*
> HEBREWS 10:24-25 (ESV)

As I read this, I had a much better and clearer understanding of why my family and I were struggling with overwhelming disillusionment, along with so many others we know who have walked away from the Church. Alternately, I was reminded of the vision I had of the shepherds with no implements or sheep, displaying looks of perplexity. Although they had abandoned the leading of the Holy Spirit and the commandments and teachings of the Bible to conduct successful ministry with more modern and impressive business models of productivity, they were perplexed by their disorientation and obvious failure. As a result, disillusionment was had by all, and quite honestly, the spiritual and church climate in America looks grim at this point.

I will also note here that many in America are prophesying revival and awakening coming to a vibrant and alive church. I would ask, how can that be if we don't first attend to a foundation that is in disarray, with spiritual malnourishment, chaos, confusion, and, in some cases, blatant disobedience and defiance? What would we, the current church, do with a revival and awakening of people coming into the current church, needing all the components to grow and thrive, when the church is in such a place of incompetence?

Disillusioned

Humility is the displacement of self by the enthronement of God.

ANDREW MURRAY,
*HUMILITY: THE JOURNEY
TOWARD HOLINESS*

CHAPTER 8

The Prodigal

The Parable of the Prodigal Son

*And he said, "There was a man who had two sons. And the
younger of them said to his father, 'Father, give me the share
of property that is coming to me.' And he divided his property
between them. Not many days later, the younger son gathered
all he had and took a journey into a far country, and there he
squandered his property in reckless living. And when he had
spent everything, a severe famine arose in that country, and he
began to be in need. So he went and hired himself out to one of
the citizens of that country, who sent him into his fields to feed
pigs. And he was longing to be fed with the pods that the pigs
ate, and no one gave him anything.*

*"But when he came to himself, he said, 'How many of my father's
hired servants have more than enough bread, but I perish here
with hunger! I will arise and go to my father, and I will say to
him, "Father, I have sinned against heaven and before you.
I am no longer worthy to be called your son. Treat me as one
of your hired servants."' And he arose and came to his father.
But while he was still a long way off, his father saw him and
felt compassion, and ran and embraced him and kissed him.
And the son said to him, 'Father, I have sinned against heaven*

and before you. I am no longer worthy to be called your son.'
But the father said to his servants, 'Bring quickly the best robe,
and put it on him, and put a ring on his hand, and shoes on his
feet. For this my son was dead, and is alive again; he was lost,
and is found.' And they began to celebrate.
LUKE 15:11-24 (ESV)

The story of the Prodigal Son is well known to many believers.
We refer to it when we are crying out for a wayward son or daughter.
We use the story in Christian teachings to illustrate the love and
forgiveness of a loving Father. The story offers a variety of beneficial
teachings regarding God's promises and principles.

The story also points to God's rebellious and defiant children
throughout the Old and New Testaments. Defiance and disobedience
started with Adam and Eve in the garden when they ate of the
forbidden fruit (Genesis 3). The story of Lot and his family taking
a different direction and separating from Abraham and his family,
due to their combined size, resulted in Lot's family adopting a
lukewarm attitude toward God. That family found itself in chaos,
disarray, rebellion, and defiance, all of which led to destruction for
themselves and a harmful influence on future generations (Genesis 19).
And then the story of Moses leading the Hebrews out of Egypt
(Exodus 3–14). And, of course, the story of the Hebrews demanding
a king from Samuel so they could be like the other nations (1 Samuel 8).
Many of the kings then led the people astray, or the people rebelled
and chased after foreign gods, and the kings followed. The Old
Testament is filled with stories of rebellion, disobedience, defiance,
and rejection of their God.

The Prodigal

"Do everything they say to you," the LORD replied, "for they are rejecting Me, not you. They don't want Me to be their king any longer."
1 SAMUEL 8:7 (NLT)

The New Testament gave us examples of Jesus being rejected. His teachings were laughed at and condemned by the Pharisees. They knew better. They knew more. They were the ones rich in understanding, tradition, and religion that fed their selfishness and pride. Thus, the Parable of the Prodigal Son.

How are we, the children of God, any different today? We fully understand there are serious faults among the church leadership of today. There is no end to self-centeredness, egos, pride, arrogance, greed and notoriety, misguided motivations, and a consuming desire for control, among other things. I've noted that in previous chapters. But what about the individual Christian who sits in the sanctuary as part of the congregation every Sunday, the sheep?

There is an underlying, and sometimes overt, attitude among Christians that presents in immature and extremely minor ways, while other times in bold and aggressive measures. I've watched wars take place in congregations that divided the congregation over simple things like the color of the carpet, what time services ended, who gets to be on a given committee, and so on. Those things are petty human-nature issues and will likely exist until the end of time. What about more serious issues that corrupt the heart and compromise the spirit?

We want to be entertained and made as comfortable as possible. We want our lattes to take to our cushy chairs as we lean back and enjoy the show, and listen to a message that makes us feel good. Bottom line, we want what we want. We are self-centered and prioritize self at all costs, subtly and overtly.

> *"Listen, O heavens, and give ear, O earth, for the LORD has spoken: 'I have raised children and brought them up, but they have rebelled against Me.'"*
> *ISAIAH 1:2 (KJV, ADAPTED)*

We see the same today. God's children are still rebelling. Antonyms of rebellion include obedience, compliance, and submission. Obedience would include applying and living according to God's Word. Compliance would invite aligning with His principles, commandments, and teachings. Submission would suggest abiding by God's leading, directing, and will. How many of us read, study, and ponder God's Word regularly, daily with desire and passion, understanding this is one of the ways to know our Lord intimately and His will for us?

> *"Study and do your best to present yourself to God approved, a workman [tested by trial] who has no reason to be ashamed, accurately handling and skillfully teaching the word of truth."*
> *2 TIMOTHY 2:15 (AMP)*

Regular Bible reading

A third of Americans who attend a Protestant church regularly (32%) say they read the Bible personally every day. Around a quarter (27%) say they read it a few times a week. Fewer say they only read it once a week (12%), a few times a month (11%), or once a month (5%). Close to 1 in 8 (12%) admit they rarely or never read the Bible.
—Lifeway Research, *Churchgoer Views and Practices*

Or...

How often do we have time to meet together for study, fellowship, prayer, and worship?

> *"Let us not neglect meeting together, as some have made a habit, but let us encourage one another, and all the more as you see the Day approaching."*
> HEBREWS 10:25 (BSB)

What Percent of Church Members Attend Regularly

There has been a significant decline in church attendance since the turn of the 21st century, according to multiple surveys from several research institutions. What percentage of churchgoing people attend regularly depends on your threshold for what you consider regular attendance. If "regular" means once a week, only 20% of Americans attend at that rate, down from 32% in 2000. If "regular" means once a month or more, the number rises to 41% *(combining those who answered weekly, almost every week, and about once a month in the Gallup survey).*

Key statistics

- 20% of Americans attend church every week *(Gallup)*
- 41% of Americans attend monthly or more *(Gallup)*
- 57% of Americans seldom or never attend religious services *(Gallup)*
- Regular church attendance has steadily declined since the turn of the century *(Gallup and Pew Research Center)*

We are less inclined to attend services regularly, which would include a weekly service. We are too busy. We find ourselves shallow, lacking spiritual knowledge, and unwilling to participate in the pursuit of a deeper relationship with our Father God, either privately or corporately.

Those lost traits are also reflected by the tithing reports. Although different sites reported varying numbers, all were low, as evidenced by this one: According to Overflow (an online reporting agency), only 5–10% of church attendees follow traditional tithing behavior. Sources: Gallup; Pew Research Center; Overflow.

Or,

Volunteer service within the church organization:
Barna has observed this mindset among practicing Christians for some time. In a 2019 Barna study, just one in five practicing

Christians pointed to financial giving as the way they most frequently express their generosity. Instead, service or volunteering was the most common expression of generosity among practicing Christians (31%). Emotional and relational support (25%) also exceeded monetary support as a method of generosity. *(Barna, 2019)*

And yet we declare our Christianity as though it were priority one often. We, like the Old Testament Israelites and New Testament Pharisees, are religious… so very religious. We claim all the rights, promote our less-than-elementary understanding of the Word of God, and wear our spiritual arrogance like a fraternity/sorority pin on our spiritual lapel. All the while, we smugly stand rather than humbly kneel in prayer; we busy ourselves with self-important matters, rather than devoting ourselves to study and discipleship; and we cater to the almighty "god of self," rather than surrender to the God of Gods.

I have a close relative who will, on occasion, engage in conversation regarding "religion," attempting to quote scripture as a weapon, only to botch the scripture reference, simply because he has heard it over the years, not read and absorbed it. That's always an entertaining conversation. We are notorious for using scripture as a weapon when we want to chastise or condemn someone.

Obviously, there is a place for pointing to scripture to support our opposition or to point out to another the consequences of their actions, but how much more effective when we use scripture and Biblical principles to encourage and draw away from sin and consequence? And rather than use scripture as a weapon to win an argument and promote our hypocrisy, we use scripture and God's principles to draw others into a beautiful and meaningful relationship with a Magnificent Father God.

I am intrigued by the words of John to the seven churches in the Book of Revelation. Only two of the seven were recognized as true followers and servants of the Most High God without reprimands and harsh criticisms.

Message to the Church in Ephesus

*"I know your works, your toil and your patient endurance, and how you cannot bear with those who are evil, but have tested those who call themselves apostles and are not, and found them to be false. I know you are enduring patiently and bearing up for my name's sake, and you have not grown weary. **But I have this against you, that you have abandoned the love you had at first. Remember therefore from where you have fallen; repent, and do the works you did at first. If not, I will come to you and remove your lampstand from its place, unless you repent.** Yet this you have: you hate the works of the Nicolaitans, which I also hate. He who has an ear, let him hear what the Spirit says to the churches. To the one who conquers I will grant to eat of the tree of life, which is in the paradise of God."* REVELATION 2:2–7 (ESV)

Message to the Church in Smyrna

"I know your tribulation and your poverty (but you are rich) and the slander of those who say that they are Jews and are not, but are a synagogue of Satan. Do not fear what you are about to suffer. Behold, the devil is about to throw some of you into prison, that you may be tested, and for ten days you will have tribulation. Be faithful unto death, and I will give you the crown of life. He who has an ear, let him hear what the Spirit says to the churches. The one who conquers will not be hurt by the second death." Revelation 2:9–11 (ESV)

Message to the Church in Pergamum

"'I know where you dwell, where Satan's throne is. Yet you hold fast my name, and you did not deny my faith even in the days of Antipas my faithful witness, who was killed among you, where Satan dwells. But I have a few things against you: you have some there who hold the teaching of Balaam, who taught Balak to put a stumbling block before the sons of Israel, so that they might eat food sacrificed to idols and practice sexual immorality. So also you have some who hold the teaching of the Nicolaitans. Therefore repent. If not, I will come to you soon and war against them with the sword of my mouth. He who has an ear, let him hear what the Spirit says to the churches. To the one who conquers I will give some of the hidden manna, and I will give him a white stone, with a new name written on the stone that no one knows except the one who receives it.'" Revelation 2:13–17 (ESV)

Message to the Church in Thyatira

"'I know your works, your love and faith and service and patient endurance, and that your latter works exceed the first. But I have this against you, that you tolerate that woman Jezebel, who calls herself a prophetess and is teaching and seducing my servants to practice sexual immorality and to eat food sacrificed to idols. I gave her time to repent, but she refuses to repent of her sexual immorality. Behold, I will throw her onto a sickbed, and those who commit adultery with her I will throw into great tribulation, unless they repent of her works, and I will strike her children dead. And all the churches will know that I am he who searches mind and heart, and I will give to each of you according to your works. But to the rest of you in Thyatira, who do not hold this teaching, who have not learned what some call the deep things of Satan, to you I say, I do not lay on you any other burden. Only hold fast what you have until I come. The one who conquers and who keeps my works until the end, to him I will give authority over the nations,'"
REVELATION 2:19–26 (ESV)

Message to the Church in Sardis

"'I know your works. You have the reputation of being alive, but you are dead. Wake up, and strengthen what remains and is about to die, for I have not found your works complete in the sight of my God. Remember, then, what you received and heard. Keep it, and repent. If you will not wake up, I will come like a thief, and you will not know at what hour I will come against you. Yet you have still a few names in Sardis, people who have not soiled their garments, and they will walk with me in white, for they are worthy. The one who conquers will be clothed thus in white garments, and I will never blot his name out of the book of life. I will confess his name before my Father and before his angels.'"
REVELATION 3:1–5 (ESV)

Message to the Church in Philadelphia

"And to the angel of the church in Philadelphia write: 'The words of the holy one, the true one, who has the key of David, who opens and no one will shut, who shuts and no one opens.

"'I know your works. Behold, I have set before you an open door, which no one is able to shut. I know that you have but little power, and yet you have kept my word and have not denied my name. Behold, I will make those of the synagogue of Satan who say that they are Jews and are not, but lie— behold, I will make them come and bow down before your feet, and they will learn that I have loved you. Because you

have kept my word about patient endurance, I will keep you from the hour of trial that is coming on the whole world, to try those who dwell on the earth. I am coming soon. Hold fast what you have, so that no one may seize your crown. The one who conquers, I will make him a pillar in the temple of my God. Never shall he go out of it, and I will write on him the name of my God, and the name of the city of my God, the new Jerusalem, which comes down from my God out of heaven, and my own new name. He who has an ear, let him hear what the Spirit says to the churches.'''
REVELATION 3:7–13 (ESV)

Message to the Church in Laodicea

"'I know your works: you are neither cold nor hot. Would that you were either cold or hot! So, because you are lukewarm, and neither hot nor cold, I will spit you out of my mouth. For you say, 'I am rich, I have prospered, and I need nothing,' not realizing that you are wretched, pitiable, poor, blind, and naked. I counsel you to buy from me gold refined by fire, so that you may be rich, and white garments so that you may clothe yourself and the shame of your nakedness may not be seen, and salve to anoint your eyes, So that you may see.

Those whom I love, I reprove and discipline, so be zealous and repent. Behold, I stand at the door and knock. If anyone hears my voice and opens the door, I will come in to him and eat with him, and he with me. The one who conquers, I will grant him

to sit with me on my throne, as I also conquered and sat down
with my Father on his throne.
REVELATION *3:15–21 (ESV)*

Note the specific sins in each of the churches charged with sin:

- **Ephesus** had abandoned their "first love."
- **Pergamum** engaged in eating food sacrificed to idols and sexual immorality.
- **Thyatira** embraced the Jezebel spirit, along with eating food sacrificed to idols and sexual immorality.
- **Sardis** had a reputation for being alive, but they were dead.
- **Laodicea** was charged with being lukewarm, or as we discovered, the synonym "casual."
- **Smyrna and Philadelphia** were the two without charges of sin, disobedience, and defiance against them.

It is also worth noting that although the Lord charged each of the five churches with disobedience, defiance, rebellion, disregard, and other sins fueled by self-centeredness, He also made it clear that if they repented and conquered, they could experience the following:

- **Ephesus**: "To the one who conquers I will grant to eat of the tree of life, which is in the paradise of God."
- **Pergamum**: "To the one who conquers I will give some of the hidden manna, and I will give him a white stone, with a new name written on the stone that no one knows except the one who receives it."
- **Thyatira**: "The one who conquers and who keeps my works until the end, to him I will give authority over the nations."

- **Sardis**: "The one who conquers will be clothed thus in white garments, and I will never blot his name out of the book of life. I will confess his name before my Father and before his angels."
- **Laodicea**: "The one who conquers, I will grant him to sit with me on my throne…"

In spite of the many sins and rejection of God and His Word, He continually offers forgiveness and restoration. What a glorious God.

Would anyone argue that the American Church of today isn't riddled with the same sins the seven churches were charged with? Sexual sin in the church is rampant. Casual sex between two consenting adults is considered acceptable by many Christians, as noted by Pew Research Center:

Half of Christians say casual sex, defined in the survey as sex between consenting adults who are not in a committed romantic relationship, is sometimes or always acceptable. Six in ten Catholics (62%) take this view, as do 56% of Protestants in the historically Black tradition, 54% of mainline Protestants, and 36% of evangelical Protestants. (Oct. 2019)

And we have stats, although a little outdated, on abortion use in the church. Research has consistently shown that the majority of people who obtain an abortion have a religious affiliation. According to the most recent Guttmacher Institute data, in 2014:

- 17% of abortion patients identified as mainline Protestant
- 13% as evangelical Protestant
- 24% as Catholic

Pew Research Center polled Christians in 2024 regarding whether abortion should be legal or illegal and found these results:

- White Evangelical Protestant: 25% legal vs. 75% illegal
- White Non-evangelical Protestant: 64% legal vs. 33% illegal
- Black Protestant: 71% legal vs. 26% illegal
- Catholic: 59% legal vs. 40% illegal

We know that pornography is widespread in the church. Recently, the percentage of women users has increased.

Since Barna's 2015 study *The Porn Phenomenon*, the number of U.S. adults consuming pornography has continued to rise, with a six-percentage point increase (from 55% in 2015 to 61% presently). There is also a notable uptick in the number of women accessing pornographic content (39% then vs. 44% now). (Barna Group, Oct. 2024)

Porn use is often a silent habit done in isolation.

Despite its widespread nature, the vast majority of porn users (84%) say no one is helping them avoid pornography, and half say no one knows about their habit. (Barna Group, Oct. 2024)

Christians are not immune to the pervasive influence of pornography.

Just over half of practicing Christians report consuming porn with some level of frequency, including 22 percent who view it weekly (15%) or daily (7%). Though numbers climb among nonpracticing

Christians and non-Christians, the reality is that a slight majority of all Christians has some sort of history of engaging with pornographic material. (Barna Group, Oct. 2024)

Premarital and illicit sex is a thriving pastime and issue in the Christian community. The consequences that align with premarital and illicit sex are numerous and disastrous. Abortion, illegitimate children, STIs, broken hearts, confused principles and convictions, inability to connect and commit long-term, and more are a few of the consequences of casual relationships.

Our sins and preoccupations today might differ in some ways from New Testament times. For instance, I don't know that we battle eating food offered first to idols, but we do battle idols of every kind. Whereas the New Testament believers were warned to avoid sexual sin, eating food offered to idols, lukewarmness, and other sins, today we deal with a broader variety of targeted and destructive sins that are wreaking havoc in the church and its participants.

When we begin to identify the sins that entangle us, we consistently discover that at the root of sin is the key motivator of self. Self wants what it wants at all costs. Self is greedy, full of lust, and consumed with the worship of self, our greater god, our greatest idol. If given its way, self will go to any length to accomplish its wishes.

How many pastors have fallen due to lust, sexual deviance, or greed? How many churches split due to division over doctrine, finances, or other silly differences? Consider the huge split in the United Methodist Church over sexual deviance and aligning with liberal social issues that was so destructive. They aren't the only denomination that has fractured and sent out shock waves in the Christian community, again causing confusion, disorientation, and abandonment of Christianity. All of the destructive and divisive issues in the life of Christianity default to selfishness, pride, arrogance, and control.

The prodigal son wanted what he wanted. He wanted it his way. He wanted more. He wanted better. He ultimately "squandered his property in reckless living."

Carpenter's Home Church in Lakeland, FL, was once a thriving and popular church that hosted many popular Christian speakers and performers. At its peak, it claimed nearly 7,000 worshipers in the early 90s. Many of us would travel the distance from the East Coast in Florida, where we lived, to attend some of those amazing services. Sadly, their popularity and successes were never enough, it seems. Arrogance and pride seeped in, and in short order, the pastor's son was charged with and convicted of fraud charges that swindled investors of millions. Over time, the church membership dwindled and was sold to another ministry, which was also burdened by debt and ultimately led to bankruptcy, causing the church campus to close. The campus was soon after demolished, and what was once a beacon of light in the community and beyond, ceased to glow.

The motivation of the prodigal son, the ministers and ministries that falter and fail after great success, and the individual Christian that falls into the trap of wanting what he or she wants are all guilty of submitting to the god of self who has elevated himself above the Father and His Word. It's always a trip that ends in disaster.

If we take another look at the seven churches, they all represent the church of today. The American Church is full of self-centeredness that presents itself in compromise, complacency, apathy, greed, arrogance, pride, casualness, and an underlying air of superiority, believing we can ultimately do it better than our Creator.

The good news, and there is always good news, is that when the prodigal went home, the Father was waiting with open arms. In each case with five of the seven churches, the Lord offered redemption and provision to those who repented and conquered. His offerings included: to eat of the tree of life, hidden manna, authority, names written in the Book of Life, and to sit with Him on His throne. Forgiveness is the greatest gift our God offers, with many other gifts added.

> *"If we confess our sins, he is faithful and just to forgive us*
> *our sins and to cleanse us from all unrighteousness."*
> *1 JOHN 1:9 (ESV)*

The Prodigal

Her eyes were opened
to the fact that right down
in the depths of her own
heart she really had but
one passionate desire,
not for the things which the
Shepherd had promised,
but for Himself.

All she wanted was
to be allowed to follow
Him forever.

HANNAH HURNARD,
HINDS FEET ON HIGH PLACES

CHAPTER 9

All is Well

Elisha and the Woman from Shunem

One day Elisha went on to Shunem, where a wealthy woman lived, who urged him to eat some food. So whenever he passed that way, he would turn in there to eat food.

And she said to her husband, "Behold now, I know that this is a holy man of God who is continually passing our way. Let us make a small room on the roof with walls and put there for him a bed, a table, a chair, and a lamp, so that whenever he comes to us, he can go in there."

One day he came there, and he turned into the chamber and rested there. And he said to Gehazi his servant, "Call this Shunammite." When he had called her, she stood before him. And he said to him, "Say now to her, 'See, you have taken all this trouble for us; what is to be done for you? Would you have a word spoken on your behalf to the king or to the commander of the army?'"

She answered, "I dwell among my own people."

And he said, "What then is to be done for her?"

Gehazi answered, "Well, she has no son, and her husband is old."

He said, "Call her." And when he had called her, she stood in the doorway. And he said, "At this season, about this time next year, you shall embrace a son."

And she said, "No, my lord, O man of God; do not lie to your servant."

But the woman conceived, and she bore a son about that time the following spring, as Elisha had said to her.

When the child had grown, he went out one day to his father among the reapers. And he said to his father, "Oh, my head, my head!"

The father said to his servant, "Carry him to his mother."

And when he had lifted him and brought him to his mother, the child sat on her lap till noon, and then he died. And she went up and laid him on the bed of the man of God and shut the door behind him and went out.

Then she called to her husband and said, "Send me one of the servants and one of the donkeys, that I may quickly go to the man of God and come back again."

And he said, "Why will you go to him today? It is neither new moon nor Sabbath."

She said, "All is well."

Then she saddled the donkey, and she said to her servant, "Urge the animal on; do not slacken the pace for me unless I tell you."

So she set out and came to the man of God at Mount Carmel. When the man of God saw her coming, he said to Gehazi his servant, "Look, there is the Shunammite. Run at once to meet her and say to her, 'Is all well with you? Is all well with your husband? Is all well with the child?'"

And she answered, "All is well."

And when she came to the mountain to the man of God, she caught hold of his feet. And Gehazi came to push her away. But the man of God said, "Leave her alone, for she is in bitter distress, and the LORD has hidden it from me and has not told me."

Then she said, "Did I ask my lord for a son? Did I not say, 'Do not deceive me?'"

He said to Gehazi, "Tie up your garment and take my staff in your hand and go. If you meet anyone, do not greet him, and if anyone greets you, do not reply. And lay my staff on the face of the child."

Then the mother of the child said, "As the LORD lives and as you yourself live, I will not leave you."

So he arose and followed her.

Gehazi went on ahead and laid the staff on the face of the child, but there was no sound or sign of life. Therefore he returned to meet him and told him, "The child has not awakened."

When Elisha came into the house, he saw the child lying dead on his bed. So he went in and shut the door behind the two of them and prayed to the LORD.

Then he went up and lay on the child, putting his mouth on his mouth, his eyes on his eyes, and his hands on his hands. And as he stretched himself upon him, the flesh of the child became warm.

Then he got up again and walked once back and forth in the house, and went up and stretched himself upon him. The child sneezed seven times, and the child opened his eyes.

Then he summoned Gehazi and said, "Call this Shunammite." So he called her.

And when she came to him, he said, "Pick up your son."

She came and fell at his feet, bowing to the ground. Then she picked up her son and went out.

2 KINGS 4:8–37 (ESV)

The introduction in my Bible to 2 Kings states this:

"In the book of 2 Kings, we read of evil rulers, rampant idolatry, and a complacent people. Despite the pressure to conform, to turn from the Lord and to serve only self, a minority of chosen people moved in the opposite direction, toward God."
(TYNDALE LIFE APPLICATION STUDY BIBLE NLT)

Those times are in many regards like our times today. They point to, in a variety of settings, the priority of serving Self, complacency toward the Lord and His Word, idolatry, and other rebellions and defiance.

Each time I read the account of the Shunammite woman, I am captivated by her core. In addition, it paints another story of God's sincerity, His blessings, intervention, and provision when faithfulness, trust, and obedience are submitted to Him. Please consider....

The Shunammite woman offered lodging and food when the Man of God was in town. The account doesn't suggest she was looking for a return on her thoughtfulness and generosity. She was just offering her faithfulness and doing what she believed was the right thing to do as an opportunity to serve presented itself. Even when she was asked, *"What is to be done for you?"* (vs. 13), she did not respond with a request. Rather, she indicated she was fine.

As we continue with the story, we are shocked that her young son... her gift from the Lord...suddenly became ill and died. Again, she didn't respond as we would expect the mother of a young son who has just died in her arms to act. She was resolute and singular in thought and action. She would see the One True God by way of His representative, Elisha, and she would not be deterred in her pursuit. She knew what her God could do. I venture to suggest, she was so concrete in her convictions and understanding of her God, she anticipated wholeheartedly the outcome.

Once she made her way to see the Man of God, her representation of God, she was not willing to settle for anything less than her full expectations to play out. Thereby, Elisha would travel with her and address the situation himself. She would have nothing to do with second best, being Gehazi. It seems clear, due to her faith and her resolve, her son was restored to life. Her gift from the Lord was placed back into her arms and life.

> *"Give careful thought to the paths for your feet and be steadfast*
> *in all your ways. Do not turn to the right or the left; keep your*
> *foot from evil."*
> PROVERBS 4:26-27 (NIV)

The Shunammite woman seemed to have an intuitive understanding of the Proverb. In her core was a steadfastness that kept her focus on her devotion. As we read the accounts of 1 and 2 Kings, we find a few others like her who represented the "remnant" of God's people in an ungodly and turbulent time. Today, we also have a "remnant" of people like her.

In spite of all the chaos, compromise, lukewarmness/casualness, rebellion, and defiance of today, that remnant is alive and well and powerful. There are those who stand out head and shoulders above others and are recognized for their ministry of leading and encouraging the remnant. They have their place in the overall picture.

I would suggest, however, the more influential…the more diligent and powerful…the more faithful are the ones that will never be known on a larger scale. They are the ones standing firmly on their feet, while kneeling before the Lord for untold hours. They are the ones reciting the Word of God and declaring it into existence for its influence in the spiritual realm. They are the ones speaking one-on-

one to another who is struggling along the way. They minister with encouragement, accountability, supports of tenderness, kindness, patience, endurance, and deep love.

There is a ground swelling of a few in number, comparatively, that are staunch in their assignments. Their faces will likely never flash on the TV screen, nor will they be mentioned in books giving accolades to their accomplishments and endeavors, nor will they stand on a stage receiving honors and recognition. But they are here among us. They are fasting, praying, ministering, sacrificing, and serving. They are the watchman…the intercessors…the servant reaching the untold needs day in and day out faithfully.

I speak of the 85-year-old widow who has children, grandchildren, and great-grandchildren. She wakes early in the morning with her requests in hand, crying out to the Lord for those she loves so. She follows with her faithful cries for her church, life group, friends, neighbors, community, country and leaders, and then globally. She has a map of the world on the wall, and each morning she prays for a different country or region and the persecuted church under attack in that area. She takes authority over the enemy. Frail and small as she is, she is powerful and mighty as she looks to the Heavens.

Or the parent that is awakened in the middle of the night to intercede to the point of exhaustion for that prodigal who resides in continual crisis.

I also point to the all-so-small prayer group that meets twice weekly and led by one who has been suffering with extensive, debilitating health issues for years. Her health issues do not dissuade her from leading the group of three or four as long as the Holy Spirit leads them each evening. They wade through the exhaustive list of needs and issues.

Or…

The women's prayer group, which meets every Monday at noon, to cry out over a gallon jar full of names, lists, and needs in the community and beyond. Then they move to the horrific issues in the world of addiction, mentioning names of those who seem hopeless to help, while clinging to the God of Hope. They shed tears over the child in an abusive home, those imprisoned in sex trafficking. They come against the forces of evil and death in abortion camps, and the lists go on and on.

The woman who faithfully, year after year, mails out many upon many birthday and get-well cards with a personal note, including an appropriate scripture or two, to minister to the one who might not receive anything from anyone else.

The man who befriends the town simpleton—a low-functioning man with an extremely low IQ resulting from inbreeding, who can't drive or, in many regards, fend for himself. The man takes him to church each Sunday, helps him at the grocery store, or drives him to a doctor's appointment to note a few helpful things. For years, the man was faithful and dependable, meeting the practical needs of the one others disregarded. No one asked him to attend to this individual who had no significant value in today's society, but they didn't need to because he understood the consuming and insatiable love the Lord had for the needy one. He understood that the simpleton was his brother in Christ and needed him. Attending to those needs was an honor that he could serve with love.

Those who risk their lives repeatedly and constantly to fight for the unborn in front of an abortion clinic, or devise plans to intercept those who are victims of human trafficking. And those who serve continually in a food kitchen or share the gospel on a street corner, or the lone warrior delivering necessities to the homeless strays on the sidewalk.

Most of these will never see the full results of their efforts in the ongoing war this side of eternity. They continue day after day, faithfully on their faces before the God of Gods, or committed to their daily acts of service, like the Shunammite woman. They are resolute in their convictions and courage to remain staunch in their battle formation!

Because of these, we can say, "ALL IS WELL." Though the earth may fall apart at the seams tomorrow, God is still on the Throne. His servants are focused. His Will will be done...on earth as it is in Heaven.

There is more to the story of the Shunammite Woman...

The Shunammite's Land Restored

Now Elisha had said to the woman whose son he had restored to life, "Arise, and depart with your household, and sojourn wherever you can, for the Lord has called for a famine, and it will come upon the land for seven years."

So the woman arose and did according to the word of the man of God. She went with her household and sojourned in the land of the Philistines seven years.

And at the end of the seven years, when the woman returned from the land of the Philistines, she went to appeal to the king for her house and her land.

Now the king was talking with Gehazi, the servant of the man of God, saying, "Tell me all the great things that Elisha has done."

And while he was telling the king how Elisha had restored the dead to life, behold, the woman whose son he had restored to life appealed to the king for her house and her land.

And Gehazi said, "My lord, O king, here is the woman, and here is her son whom Elisha restored to life."

And when the king asked the woman, she told him.

So the king appointed an official for her, saying, "Restore all that was hers, together with all the produce of the fields from the day that she left the land until now."

2 KINGS 8:1–6 (ESV)

The Shunammite lived her life with one core purpose... she would be obedient and devoted. When the difficulties became so extreme, Elisha advised her and her family to move to escape the famine, and she obeyed. We don't know if her husband was still alive, but we do understand she was the spiritual receptionist in the family. She was also exact in her responses and obedience—she left for the full seven years trusting Elisha with the timeline.

And where did she and her family retreat to? She and her household sojourned in the land of the Philistines. To *sojourn* means to take up temporary residence. She and her family lived among the enemy until the famine was over, and, obviously, they were sustained for the seven years they were there. When the famine was over, she returned to hopefully claim her property. Again, because of her stanch devotion, the king was prompted, supernaturally by the Lord, to return to her all that was hers, together with all the produce of the fields from the day that she left the land until she presented herself.

There are three significant events to be emphasized in this story. As already noted, the Shunammite Woman was devout, sincere, with no division in her motives and convictions. The first issue was that she had no child, which meant that should her husband pass away, she would have no one to care for her, often meaning widows starved to death. She was content with her circumstances when she had no children, and yet, she expressed great joy and humility when Elisha prophesied a child to her.

The second issue came after her son was born. She embraced and nurtured the child, and when he was suddenly taken, she didn't react emotionally, but practically and responsibly. She pursued Elisha, the Man of God, to attend to her crisis. Her son was restored.

Issue number three arose when famine struck the land. She again responded with decisive obedience, relocating to the land of the enemy where there were apparent provisions. When she returned after the famine was over to reclaim her land and possessions, the story suggests that she had not compromised her faith and devotion to the Lord while living in a foreign and heathen land. In every situation or crisis, she kept her focus intact, directed on the Lord and her faith and trust in Him.

The principle laid out in the story of the Shunammite Woman is clear: if we are devoted to a fault with no ulterior motives, the Lord's favor, blessings, provisions, direction, and protection are always with us, as evidenced in this story. Imagine being that resolute in your core.

> *"Blessed are all who fear the Lord, who walk in obedience to him."*
> *PSALMS 128:1 (NIV)*

Or...

> *"This is what I told them: 'Obey me, and I will be your God, and you will be my people. Do everything as I say, and all will be well!'"*
> *JEREMIAH 7:23 (NLT)*

Or...

> *"He replied, 'Blessed rather are those who hear the word of God and obey it.'"*
> *LUKE 11:28 (NIV)*

Once again, I strongly suggest the modern-day American church is in shambles. Many—if not most—pastors preach a feel-good message that feeds self-centeredness. Their personal convictions are compromised, if not corrupt. Church denominations are primarily concerned with their man-made positions, doctrines, and theologies. Those who attend church often want nothing more than to check off a box on their to-do list.

While sitting in the sanctuary, listening to a sermon, their thoughts and interests often drift to the golf course, or they wonder how the football game later in the afternoon will play out. Most have more enthusiasm for the coming ball game than for the opportunity to sit in the House of God with brothers and sisters, participating in a service.

We are repeating a cycle that has had many revolutions before our time—and if the Lord tarries, it will likely complete another cycle, or two, or three. We don't know when the Lord will return—only that He will. So why discuss this? For many reasons. We are called to do all we know to do in any given opportunity, and then stand.

> *"Therefore take up the full armor of God, so that when the day of evil comes, you will be able to stand your ground, and having done everything, to stand."*
> EPHESIANS 6:13 (BSB)

For those of us who are willing and desirous to be as devoted and surrendered as the Shunammite woman, we look at the times we are in and join the remnant to play our part. In reality, these are exciting and invigorating times. We get to be involved, take our place in the

Army of God, accept our assignments, and charge forward with all the energy, enthusiasm, and passion afforded us as we unify with others while aligning with the Master Commander. In the midst of this roller coaster of a ride, we declare:

"All is well!"

All is Well

O Jerusalem, I have posted
watchmen on your walls;
they will pray day and
night, continually.
Take no rest, all you who
pray to the LORD.
Give the LORD no rest until
He completes His work,
until He makes Jerusalem
the pride of the earth..

Isaiah 62:6-7 (NLT)

CHAPTER 10

In Closing...
Our Lavish and Extravagant God!

"When someone has been given much, much will be required in return; and when someone has been entrusted with much, even more will be required."
LUKE 12:48 (NLT)

The principle is crystal clear in this Scripture. To be sure we understand what a principle is in the Scriptures, let's look at the definition. Merriam-Webster defines it as follows:

Principle
1: a comprehensive and fundamental law, doctrine, or assumption
B (1): a rule or code of conduct
(2): habitual devotion to right principles

I have discovered, through years of reading and studying my Bible, that a principle is most easily identified when you can take a Scripture, such as Luke 12:48, and apply it as read or apply it in the converse. The more one is given, much will be required in return. That's obvious. But then reverse it: To whom much is required, much will be given in return. The principle is established, and in God's Word it can't be altered or revoked, only applied or rejected. When it's understood, it offers a beauty beyond expression, and when it's applied, it provides blessings and provisions beyond imagination.

I suspect the Shunammite woman understood this principle intuitively in her core, as others throughout the Old and New Testaments did. Daniel is another who comes to mind. These two, and others, abided by their "lot in life," as we might phrase it today. It's evidenced in the following verse when Elisha called the woman in to ask what he might do for her, and in response she said:

> *When he had called her, she stood before him. And he said to him, "Say now to her, 'See, you have taken all this trouble for us; what is to be done for you? Would you have a word spoken on your behalf to the king or to the commander of the army?'" She answered, "I dwell among my own people."*
> *2 KINGS 4:12–13 (ESV)*

She indicated she had all she needed; her family provided for her. She seemed content with serving and devotion. She had all she needed. The Lord had provided for her in abundance, and she wanted to give in return as she saw need and opportunity by meeting a need for Elisha and his servant Gehazi. In return, the Lord blessed her with more: a son, an heir that she and her husband did not have.

She had been given much, and in return she gave. As she gave in return, she was blessed with more: a son. Her actions were not contrived or filled with ulterior motives. She responded with sincerity and pure motives.

Daniel Taken to Babylon

*In the third year of the reign of Jehoiakim, king of Judah,
Nebuchadnezzar, king of Babylon, came to Jerusalem and
besieged it. And the Lord gave Jehoiakim king of Judah into
his hand, with some of the vessels of the house of God.
And he brought them to the land of Shinar, to the house of
his god, and placed the vessels in the treasury of his god.*

*Then the king commanded Ashpenaz, his chief eunuch, to bring
some of the people of Israel, both of the royal family and of
the nobility: youths without blemish, of good appearance
and skillful in all wisdom, endowed with knowledge,
understanding learning, and competent to stand in the king's
palace, and to teach them the literature and language of the
Chaldeans. The king assigned them a daily portion of the food
that the king ate, and of the wine that he drank. They were to
be educated for three years, and at the end of that time they
were to stand before the king.*

*Among these were Daniel, Hananiah, Mishael, and Azariah
of the tribe of Judah. And the chief of the eunuchs gave them
names: Daniel he called Belteshazzar, Hananiah he called
Shadrach, Mishael he called Meshach, and Azariah he
called Abednego.*

Daniel's Faithfulness

But Daniel resolved that he would not defile himself with the king's food, or with the wine that he drank. Therefore, he asked the chief of the eunuchs to allow him not to defile himself. And God gave Daniel favor and compassion in the sight of the chief of the eunuchs, and the chief of the eunuchs said to Daniel, "I fear my lord the king, who assigned your food and your drink; for why should he see that you were in worse condition than the youths who are of your own age? So you would endanger my head with the king."

Then Daniel said to the steward whom the chief of the eunuchs had assigned over Daniel, Hananiah, Mishael, and Azariah, "Test your servants for ten days; let us be given vegetables to eat and water to drink. Then let our appearance and the appearance of the youths who eat the king's food be observed by you, and deal with your servants according to what you see." So he listened to them in this matter and tested them for ten days.

At the end of ten days, it was seen that they were better in appearance and fatter in flesh than all the youths who ate the king's food. So the steward took away their food and the wine they were to drink and gave them vegetables.

As for these four youths, God gave them learning and skill in all literature and wisdom, and Daniel had understanding in all visions and dreams. At the end of the time, when the

king had commanded that they should be brought in, the chief
of the eunuchs brought them in before Nebuchadnezzar.
And the king spoke with them, and among all of them none
was found like Daniel, Hananiah, Mishael, and Azariah.
Therefore, they stood before the king. And in every matter of
wisdom and understanding about which the king inquired of
them, he found them ten times better than all the magicians
and enchanters that were in all his kingdom. And Daniel was
there until the first year of King Cyrus.
DANIEL 1:1–21 (ESV)

Once again, we see nothing more than absolute surrender and abiding when Daniel and others were taken captive by Nebuchadnezzar, king of Babylon. It's speculated that Daniel and the other young men were made eunuchs, as was the custom of war, when they were brought in to serve the foreign king. In addition, any hopes or dreams in their personal lives were eliminated for the rest of their lives. They would live and serve at the king's pleasure and demands. Their lives were no longer their own.

In today's Christian teachings, they would likely be counseled to first take authority over the enemy that had ransomed them into bondage. They would be encouraged to fight for their freedom, to appeal to the God of mercy and grace and intervention; to have enough faith, and they would be freed and vindicated.

And yet, in that era it was understood, if they had any sense about them, they would abide and serve. Daniel did, it seems, willingly.

He deferred to the Lord's allowances and asked only one thing that ultimately served him well. He asked that he and his friends not be required to eat the king's food so they would not be defiled. His request was made in humility and with consideration. He presented alternative foods, and if they didn't meet the prescribed standards, they would yield to the king's requirements.

As with the Shunammite woman, the Lord honored and provided for Daniel and his friends because each of them first honored and trusted the Lord by submitting to their circumstances. They knew, intuitively by faith and through their deep abiding relationship with the Lord, that He was in control and they were exactly where they were supposed to be.

The American church philosophy and teachings of today, by and large, subscribe to the "God of Self," as I have addressed in previous chapters. We seek what Self wants: what will benefit and please self, what will enhance and prosper self. How many times during prayer and conversation with the Lord do we emphasize, "Your will be done, Lord, not my will"? Most modern-day Christians would cringe at such a statement. Could they sincerely express that statement from a right place of motivation? Doubtful that it ever occurred to them.

The full scope of heretical and imbalanced teachings is filling the Church pulpits to support the need for numbers and dollars. At all costs, we keep the doors open, the dollars flowing, and the church budget supported. In essence, to do that, we tickle the ears and subscribe to self-centered religion and philosophies. In addition, we keep it brief and concise so we can herd each time-slotted congregation in and out in time for the next.

In Closing... Our Lavish and Extravagant God!

We avoid topics and phrases that will offend or contradict popular secular views and social trends. Sadly, there is rarely, if ever, in the time-constrained church an opportunity to consider approaching the altar to linger or travail. There might be an alternate location to send those who respond to a sermon so as not to hinder the almighty schedule of the day. God forbid the Holy Spirit lead and control a worship service. That interference cannot be tolerated, except possibly in a service being held by the remnant or in an underground church in areas of great persecution. How far the American church has fallen.

Both the Shunammite woman and Daniel showed us that our true draw to the Lord and being His children is not to operate in the "Name it and claim it" teachings or to subscribe to "God wants you to live your best life yet" philosophy, but rather to submit, surrender, devote, sacrifice, commit to a fault (if possible), abide, yield, and even linger in His presence.

To do so grants us a place of lavish and extravagant relationship with our Lord and Savior that looks very different than the self-centered philosophy. Imagine a relationship with the Lord so intimate, so personal, so consuming, that we take on His likeness and His character, and naturally operate in a lavish and extravagant perspective not only in the way we receive from Him, but in the way we live our lives in service and devotion.

Again, I reiterate: both the Shunammite woman and Daniel experienced the principle of receiving and giving as they yielded their lives to their God.

You might argue that Daniel's life was taken from him, and that would be true. Even so, he yielded his life wholeheartedly to the Lord, resulting in a life of magnificent testimony to the power and glory of God, along with great respect, admiration, and honor from all who knew him. He had tremendous influence throughout his life. He received great prophetic words and revelations that have impacted the world throughout time. His place in existence holds immeasurable value and will greatly affect times yet to come. Although his life was not what he might have originally planned, it exceeded any dreams and hopes he may have had on his own, living instead a *lavish and extravagant* place of existence.

We, too, can pursue a similar existence.

Spiritual Blessings in Christ

Blessed be the God and Father of our Lord Jesus Christ,
who has blessed us in Christ with every spiritual blessing
in the heavenly places, even as he chose us in him before the
foundation of the world, that we should be holy and blameless
before him. In love he predestined us for adoption to himself
as sons through Jesus Christ, according to the purpose of
his will, to the praise of his glorious grace, with which he
has blessed us in the Beloved. In him we have redemption
through his blood, the forgiveness of our trespasses, according
to the riches of his grace, which he lavished upon us, in all
wisdom and insight making known to us the mystery of his
will, according to his purpose, which he set forth in Christ

as a plan for the fullness of time, to unite all things in Christ, things in heaven and things on earth in him.

In him we have obtained an inheritance, having been predestined according to the purpose of him who works all things according to the counsel of his will, so that we who were the first to hope in Christ might be to the praise of his glory. In him you also, when you heard the word of truth, the gospel of your salvation, and believed in him, were sealed with the promised Holy Spirit, who is the guarantee of our inheritance until we acquire possession of it, to the praise of his glory.
EPHESIANS 1:3–14 (ESV)

And,

The Cheerful Giver

The point is this: whoever sows sparingly will also reap sparingly, and whoever sows bountifully will also reap bountifully. Each one must give as he has decided in his heart, not reluctantly or under compulsion, for God loves a cheerful giver. And God is able to make all grace abound to you, so that having all sufficiency in all things at all times, you may abound in every good work. As it is written, "He has distributed freely, he has given to the poor; his righteousness endures forever." He who supplies seed to the sower and bread for food will supply and multiply your seed for sowing and increase the harvest of your righteousness. You will be enriched in every

way to be generous in every way, which through us will
produce thanksgiving to God.
2 CORINTHIANS *9:6–11 (ESV)*

And,

One person is lavish yet grows still richer;
another is too sparing, yet is the poorer.
Whoever confers benefits will be amply enriched,
and whoever refreshes others will be refreshed.
PROVERBS *11:24–25 (NABRE)*

May we who profess to love and follow the Lord relinquish ourselves
to a place of complete and total surrender so that we can, in these
most unpredictable and unprecedented times, be of the same character
and quality as Daniel, the Shunammite Woman, Esther, Paul,
and so many others who set the standard for us. The time is now!
We are called, and it would be wise and prudent for us to willingly
step into all the Lord is leading us to.

Mighty Warriors of the Lord,
RISE UP AND TAKE YOUR POSITIONS!
May Revival and Awakening
consume our land!

In Closing... Our Lavish and Extravagant God!

THE CASUALNESS HAS TO GO!

EPILOGUE

One Last Comment

It is my prayer and my hope that you have not read this book as a rant, but rather as a revelation—one of great proportions. We now live in a time that requires us, and more importantly, God is calling us as His children to subscribe to a deep, deep place of abiding relationship that defers to Him rather than subscribing to the hypocritical god of self.

The time is coming, and is almost here, when each of us will be prompted and motivated in some way, great or small, to take our stand, defend our faith, and abide by the commandments and solid principles of God's Word—our manual for living this life. We have taken so much for granted. We have perverted and manipulated the Word of God to fit into and support our new religion: serving the god of self, and requiring God to be our "sugar daddy" by answering all of our greedy and self-centered prayers.

We are called to pray and to ask, but with right motives and sincere hearts. And by all means, ask to the best of our understanding, according to and in alignment with God's will in all things at all times—even if it means yielding to an enemy king and serving at his pleasure for the purpose of greater accomplishments the Lord has in mind, or moving to enemy territory for provision and protection.

I am reminded that Daniel prayed three times a day. The Shunammite woman went looking for the man of God, Elisha, and sought his intervention.

**It is time for God's children—*the remnant*—
to rise up and operate in their calling by following
the examples of the Shunammite woman and Daniel,
to name a few heroes in the Bible.**

References

Barna Group. *The Porn Phenomenon*. 2015.

Barna Group. "Generosity expressions among practicing Christians" (2019 study cited).

Barna Group. "Pornography use statistics" (October 2024 findings cited).

Gallup. "Religion" polling and trend data (as cited).

Guttmacher Institute. "Abortion patients' religious affiliation" (2014 data cited).

Krejcir, Richard J. "Why Churches Fail: Part I." *ChurchLeaders*.

Lifeway Research. "Churchgoer Views and Practices" (Bible-reading frequency cited).

Merriam-Webster. "Principle." *Merriam-Webster Dictionary*.

Overflow. "Traditional tithing behavior" (5–10% figure cited).

Pew Research Center. "Casual sex acceptability among Christians" (October 2019 findings cited).

Pew Research Center. "Christian views on whether abortion should be legal or illegal" (2024 findings cited).

Tyndale Life Application Study Bible (New Living Translation). Introduction to 2 Kings (quoted).

Bible Translations Referenced

Amplified Bible (AMP).

Berean Standard Bible (BSB).

English Standard Version (ESV).

King James Version (KJV) (as cited).

New American Bible, Revised Edition (NABRE).

New International Version (NIV).

New Living Translation (NLT).

About the Author

Sherry Huck became a Christian in 1979 at age 22 and has spent decades involved in local church life—studying Scripture, serving, and learning what faithfulness looks like in real communities. This book was written out of a longing to see the Church renewed from the inside out: hearts reclaimed, convictions strengthened, and devotion, awe, and reverence for the Lord restored.

Sherry lives in a beautiful rural area of Tennessee with her husband and two of their six children. She continues to invest in the quiet, consistent work that often goes unseen.

Thank you for reading.
If this book stirred something in you,
would you leave a quick Amazon review?
Your review helps strengthen the reach of this message.